Three Books

Books by Galway Kinnell

POETRY

What a Kingdom It Was   1960

Flower Herding on Mount Monadnock   1964

Body Rags   1968

First Poems 1946–1954   1971

The Book of Nightmares   1971

The Avenue Bearing the Initial of Christ into
    the New World   1974, 2002

Mortal Acts, Mortal Words   1980

Selected Poems   1982

The Past   1985

When One Has Lived a Long Time Alone   1990

Three Books   1993, 2002

Imperfect Thirst   1994

A New Selected Poems   2000, 2001

PROSE

Black Light   1966

Walking Down the Stairs: Selections from Interviews   1978

How the Alligator Missed Breakfast (for children)   1982

THREE BOOKS

Body Rags

Mortal Acts, Mortal Words

The Past

GALWAY KINNELL

A MARINER BOOK
Houghton Mifflin Company
BOSTON   NEW YORK   2002

FIRST MARINER BOOKS EDITION, 2002

Three Books: Copyright © 1993, 2002 by Galway Kinnell
Body Rags: Copyright © 1965, 1966, 1967 by Galway Kinnell
Mortal Acts, Mortal Words: Copyright © 1980 by Galway Kinnell
The Past: Copyright © 1985 by Galway Kinnell

For information about permission to reproduce selections from this
book, write to Permissions, Houghton Mifflin Company,
215 Park Avenue South, New York, New York 10003.

Visit our Web site at www.houghtonmifflinbooks.com.

Library of Congress Cataloging-in-Publication Data

   Kinnell, Galway, date.
    [Poems. Selections]
   Three books / Galway Kinnell.
   p. cm.
   Includes index.
   Contents: Body Rags—Mortal Acts, Mortal Words—The Past.
   ISBN 0-618-21911-0
   I. Title.
PS3521.1582A6   1993
811'.54—dc20   93-5009   CIP

Book design by Anne Chalmers
Typeface: Electra

Printed in the United States of America

QUM 10 9 8 7 6 5 4 3 2 1

AUTHOR'S NOTE

I have long wanted to bring all my poems to their finished and final form. With that in mind, I have taken, over the years, every opportunity to revise them. This new Mariner edition of *Three Books* presents me with perhaps a kind of ultimatum: now or never.

Since the poems in the original *Three Books* had already undergone a number of revisions, I expected them now to need only a little tweaking. So it turned out with most of the poems. But with a few others I confess I was startled to find at this late date so many weaknesses.

If the weaknesses now were immediately obvious to me, why was I blind to them ten years ago, in 1992, when I was preparing the text for the first edition of *Three Books*? I refer the reader to Horace's well-known pronouncement—which I mistook for comic hyperbole on first encountering it in college—that a poet must wait ten years to be able to see what he has wrought. I have come to agree with this dictum completely—I should say more than completely, for I am prepared not only to wait those ten years but also to wait another ten in case new problems turn up.

Most of the poems in this book, to my eye—and ear and mouth—seem to have contracted over the past decade only a few minor ailments, letting me at last confidently pronounce them cured. Those others, afflicted with illnesses both hard to identify and hard to remedy, which I've been struggling with so much these days, also now appear to be cured—but of that I'll know more in 2012.

Galway Kinnell
Sheffield, Vermont
January 1, 2002

CONTENTS

II

III

MORTAL ACTS, MORTAL WORDS

I

II

III

IV

THE PAST

I

II

III

Body Rags

to Inés

PART I

Another Night in the Ruins

1

In the evening
haze darkening on the hills,
purple of the eternal,
a last bird crosses over,
'*flop flop*,' adoring
only the instant.

2

Nine years ago,
in a plane that rumbled all night
above the Atlantic,
I could see, lit up
by lightning bolts jumping out of it,
a thunderhead formed like the face
of my brother, looking down
on blue,
lightning-flashed moments of the Atlantic.

3

He used to tell me,
"What good is the day?
On some hill of despair
the bonfire

you kindle can light the great sky—
though it's true, it turns out, to make it burn
you have to throw yourself in..."

4

Wind tears itself hollow
in the eaves of these ruins, ghost-flute
of snowdrifts
that build out there in the dark:
upside-down ravines
into which night sweeps
our cast wings, our ink-spattered feathers.

5

I listen.
I hear nothing. Only
the cow, the cow of such
hollowness, mooing
down the bones.

6

Is that a
rooster? He
thrashes in the snow
for a grain. Finds
it. Rips
it into

flames. Flaps. Crows.
Flames
bursting out of his brow.

7

How many nights must it take
one such as me to learn
that we aren't, after all, made
from that bird that flies out of its ashes,
that for us
as we go up in flames, our one work
is
to open ourselves, to *be*
the flames?

Lost Loves

1

On ashes of old volcanoes
I lie baking
the deathward flesh in the sun.

I can hear
a door, far away,
banging in the wind:

Mole Street. Quai-aux-Fleurs. Françoise.
Greta. "After Lunch" by Po Chu-I.
"The Sunflower" by Blake.

2

And yet I can rejoice
that everything changes, that
we go from life
into life,

and enter ourselves
quaking
like the tadpole, its time come, tumbling toward the slime.

Getting the Mail

I walk back
toward the frog pond, carrying
the one letter, a few wavy lines
crossing the stamp: tongue-streaks
leaching through
from the glue and spittle beneath: my sign.

The frogs'
eyes bulge toward the visible,
an alderfly glitters past, declining
to die: her third giant step
into the world.

A name stretches over the envelope
like a blindfold.
What did *getting warm* used to mean?

I tear open the letter
to the far-off, serene
groans of a cow
a farmer milks in the August dusk
and the Kyrie of a chainsaw drifting down off Wheelock Mountain.

Vapor Trail Reflected in the Frog Pond

1

The old watch: their
thick eyes
puff and foreclose by the moon. The young, heads
trailed by the beginnings of necks,
shiver,
in the guarantee they shall be bodies.

In the frog pond
the vapor trail of a SAC bomber creeps,

I hear its drone, drifting, high up
in immaculate ozone.

2

And I hear,
coming over the hills, America singing,
her varied carols I hear:
crack of deputies' rifles practicing their aim on stray dogs at night,
sput of cattleprod,
TV going on about the smells of the human body,
curses of the soldier as he poisons, burns, grinds, and stabs
the rice of the world,
with open mouth, crying strong, hysterical curses.

3

And by paddies in Asia
bones
wearing a few shadows
walk down a dirt road, smashed
bloodsuckers on their heel, knowing
flesh thrown down in the sunshine
dogs shall eat
and flesh flung into the air
shall be seized by birds,
shoulder blades smooth, unmarked by old feather-holes,
hands rivered
by blue, erratic wanderings of the blood,
eyes crinkled shut at almost seeing
the drifting sun that gives us our lives.

The Fossils

1

I clawed in the crushed-up
lumps half grease half dust:
atrypas came out,
lophophyllidiums still casting shadows,
corals wrapped in wrinkles,
wing-shaped allorismas,
sea-lily disks that did not molder into dust
but held.

Night rose up
in black smoke, making me
blind. My fingertips rasped
smooth on my brain, I knelt in the dark, cracking
the emptiness: poking
spirifers into flying black dust,
letting sylvan remains slither through my fingers,
whiffing the glacial roses,
palping around for the ephemera.

Will I touch at last
the ornithosuchus, whose wings
serve not to evade earth but to press closer to it?

2

While Bill Gratwick flapped, pranced
and called the dances,
light-headed
as a lizard on hind legs I sashayed
with Sylvia, of the woods, as woodwinds
flared and crackled in the leaves,
Sylph-ia, too, of that breeze
for whom even the salamander rekindles wings;
and I danced the eighteenth-century shoulder-rub
with Lucy,
my shoulder blades starting to glitter
on hers as we turned, sailbacks
in laired and changing dance,
our faces smudged with light from the fingertips of the ages.

3

Outside
in dark fields
I pressed the coiled
ribs of a fingerprint to a stone,
first light in the flesh.

Over the least fossil
day breaks in gold, frankincense, and myrrh.

The Burn

On the dirt road winding
beside the Kilchis River
down to the sea, saplings
on all the hills, I go
deep into the first forest
of Douglas firs shimmering
out of prehistory, a strange
shine up where the tops
shut out the sky, whose roots
feed in the waters of the rainbow trout.
And here, at my feet, in the grain
of a burnt log opened by a riverfall,
the swirls of the creation.
At the San Francisco airport,
Charlotte, where yesterday
my arms died around you like
old snakeskins, needletracks
on your arms marked
how the veins wander.
I see you walking like a somnambulist
through a poppy field, blind
as myself on this dirt road, tiny
flowers brightening about you,
the skills of fire, of fanning
the blossoms until they flare and die,
perfected; only the power to nurture
and prolong, only this love,

impossible. The mouth of the river.
On these beaches
the sea throws itself down, in flames.

One Who Used to Beat His Way

Down the street of warehouses,
each with
its redlighted shaftway,
its Corinthian columns,
its bum crapped out on the stoop,
he staggers, among
wraiths that steam up out of manhole covers
and crimesheets skidding from the past.

He gets a backed-up
mouthful of liquor, mumbles, "Thanks God,"
and regulps it.
Behind him the continent glimmers, that wild land
crossed by the *Flying Crow*
that changes her crew at Shreveport,
the *Redball* and the *Dixie Flyer*, that go on through,
the *Big 80*
that quills her whistles to make blues on the Delta.
"Everybody's eating everybody,"
the old timer growls, poking the jungle fire...
"Bible-ranters, bulls, hicks, systems, scissor-bills..."

And he who used
to beat his way hauls himself down
into his sleeping niche, where he has cached his small possessions,
a nearly killed bottle,
a streambed of dried piss groping across the dry stone.

The Fly

The fly
I've just brushed
off my face keeps buzzing
about me, flesh-
eater
starved for the soul.

One day I may learn to suffer
his mizzling, sporadic stroll over eyelid or cheek,
even hear my own singing
in his burnt song.

The bee is the fleur-de-lys in the flesh.
She has a tuft of the sun on her back.
She brings sexual love to the narcissus flower.
She sings of fulfillment only
and stings and dies, and
everything she ever touches
is opening, opening.

And yet we say our last goodbye
to the fly last,
the flesh-fly last,
the absolute last,
the naked dirty reality of him last.

The Falls

The elemental murmur
as they plunge, *croal, croal,*
and *haish, haish,* over
the ledges,
through stepless wheels
and bare axles, down between
sawmills that have
slid sideways to their knees...

When I fall I would fall to my sounding...
the lowly,
unchanged, stillic, rainbowed sounding
of the Barton River Falls.

Mango

It opens in three: yellow-gold as dawn
on the mudwalls of Hafez' garden,
on a seagull mewing for the light,

austere,
smacking of turpentine,
stringy, like the mortal flesh.

Under the mango tree,
a few women squat by the whitening sea,
clapping, chorusing of love.

In the Anse Galet Valley

Clouds
rise by twos out of the jungle, cross
under the moon, sink
into
the peak called Font-des-Serpents.

I remember the game of angel's wings,
I remember the laid-open scallop shell,
the gowpen overspilling the milled grain,
a mole feeling its way through the daylight.

A straw torch
flickers
among the trees,
of a nightfisherman
wading upstream clubbing the fishes.

The fer-de-lances
writhe in black winding-skins.
What questions could I ask that wafer-
moon
gnawed already at its death-edge?

La Bagarède

1

The dogs come with me
into town, we buy chèvre and a bâtard.
Back at La Bagarède I eat
this little meal in the dusk
and sit, until

the Swan grows visible, trailing
her indicated wings down the horizon,
and Orion
begins to stalk the last nights of the summer.

2

The black
water I gulp from the spring
hits my brain at the root.
The dark blooms of sunflowers
crackle open. In the sky
the seventh
of the Sisters, she who hid herself
in shame
at having loved one who dies, is shining.

Night in the Forest

A woman
sleeps next to me. A strand
of hair flows
from her cocoon sleeping bag, touching
the ground hesitantly, as if thinking
to take root.

    ∫

A mountain brook purls,
blood winds
through its memorized labyrinths.
A few feet away
charred stick-ends surround
a bit of ashes, where flames
absently
waver, absently leap.

Going Home by Last Light

Redheaded by last light,
with high-stepped, illusionist amble
I walk toward the white room
where she will be waiting,
past
pimentos,
red cabbages,
tomatoes flickering in their bins,
past melons, past mushrooms and onions.

Those swarms
of mayflies that used to rise
at the Vermont threshold, "imagos"
thrown up for a day,
their mouths shriveling closed,
their sexual parts newborn and perfect...

For the last few minutes
two mosquitoes have been mating
on top of this poem,
changing positions, swooning,
their legs
fragile as a baby's hairs.

A day!
The wings of the earth
lift and fall
to the groans, the savage thumpings of a heart.

How Many Nights

How many nights
have I lain in terror,
O Creator Spirit, maker of night and day,

only to walk out
the next morning over the frozen world,
hearing under the creaking of snow
faint, peaceful breaths...
snake,
bear, earthworm, ant...

and above me
a wild crow crying *'yaw yaw yaw'*
from a branch nothing cried from ever in my life.

Last Songs

What do they sing, the last birds
coasting down the twilight,
banking
across woods filled with darkness, their
frayed wings curved
on the world like lovers' arms
which form, night after night, in sleep,
an irremediable absence?

୭

Silence. Ashes
in the grate. Whatever it is
that keeps us from heaven,
sloth, wrath, greed, fear,
could we only reinvent it on earth
as song.

In the Farmhouse

Eaves moan,
loose clapboards flap.

Behind me the potbellied
Ironside #120, rusty, cracked,
rips thick chunks of rock maple
into fire.

     ‽

Soon it will be spring,
Soon the vanishing of the snows.

And tonight
in this flimsy jew's-harp of a farmhouse
I sit up late, mouthing
sounds that would be words
in the wind
rattling the twelve lights of blackness.

The Correspondence School Instructor
Says Goodbye to His Poetry Students

Goodbye, lady in Bangor, who sent me
snapshots of yourself, after definitely hinting
you were beautiful; goodbye,
Miami Beach urologist, who enclosed plain
brown envelopes for the return of your *very*
"Clinical Sonnets"; goodbye, manufacturer
of brassieres on the Coast, whose eclogues
give the fullest treatment in literature yet
to the sagging breast motif; goodbye, you in San Quentin,
who wrote, "Being German my hero is Hitler,"
instead of "Sincerely yours," at the end of long,
neat-scripted letters extolling the Pre-Raphaelites:

I swear to you, it was just my way
of cheering myself up, as I licked
the stamped, self-addressed envelopes,
the game I had of trying to guess
which one of you, this time,
had poisoned his glue. I did care.
I did read each poem entire.
I did say everything I thought
in the mildest words I knew. And now,
in this poem, or chopped prose, no better,
I realize, than those troubled lines
I kept sending back to you,
I have to say I am relieved it is over:

at the end I could feel only pity
for that urge toward more life
your poems kept smothering in words, the smell
of which, days later, tingled in your nostrils
as new, God-given impulses
to write.

Goodbye,
you who are, for me, the postmarks again
of imaginary towns—Xenia, Burnt Cabins, Hornell—
their solitude given away in poems, only their loneliness kept.

The Poem

On this hill crossed
by the last birds, a sprinkling
of soil covers up the rocks
with green, as
the face
drifts on a skull scratched by glaciers.

The poem too
is a palimpsest, pinked
with erasures, smelling
of departure and burnt stone.

❧

The full moon
slides out from the clouds, the trees'
graves all lie out at their feet:

the white-oak-leaf-
shaped tongue
of the new born and the dying
quivers, and no one interprets it.

❧

Where is "The Apocalypse of Lamech"?
Where is the "Iliupersis"?
Where is the "Khavadhaynamagh"?
Where is the "Rommant du Pet au Deable"?

Where is "The Book of the Lion"?
Where is the servantose of the sixty girls of Florence?
Where are the poems Li Po folded into boats and pushed out on
    the river?
Where are the snows that fell into these graves?

_♫_

In morning light, at the tip
of an icicle, the letter C
comes into being—trembles,
to drop, or to cling?

Suddenly a roman
carapace glitters all over it.

_♫_

Here is a fern-leaf cementing *utter* to *illume,*
here is *unfulfilled* reflected as *mellifica* along the feather of a crow,
here is a lightning-split fir the lines down its good side becoming
    ever more whitmanesque and free,
here is a hound chasing a mate in trochaic dimeter
    brachycatalectic,
here are the pits where the tongue-bone is hurled at its desolate
    cry,
here are clothes held up by clothespins composing *emptiness* in
    khaskura,
here is a fly convulsing through the poisoned labyrinth of this
    handwriting,
here is an armful of last-year's-snows.

_♫_

The moment
in the late night, when baby birds
closed in dark wings almost stir, and objects
on the page grow suddenly
heavy, hugged
by an intensification of strange gravity:

the surgery of the funeral
and of the funeral oration, the absence
in the bit of speech I would leave in the world
of

　　　♫

Where are "The Onions"
heaped like swollen lachrymal sacs in a bushel basket in a grocery
　　　store
in 1948?

brong ding plang ching of a spike
driven crazy on a locust
post.

PART II

The Last River

1

When I cross
on the high, back-reared ferry
all burnished brass and laboring pistons
and admire the tugs and sticklighters
and the great ships from foreign lands
and wave to a deckhand gawking at the new world
of sugar cane and shanties and junked cars
and see a girl by the railing,
the shapes the breeze presses her dress against,
and the green waves lighting up...
the cell-block
door crawls open and they fling us a pimp.

2

The lights dim,
the dirty jokes die out.

Rumble of trailertrucks
on Louisiana 1 ... I think
of the rides
back from the courthouse in Amite,
down the canyon between
faces smiling from the billboards,
the car filled

with men and women who tried to register to vote
crawling down the canyon made
of billboards of huge, smiling, white faces ...
Tickfaw ... Independence ... Albany...
Moan of
a riverboat creeping
upstream ... yap and screech
of police dogs
attacking the police in their dreams.

3

Under the blue flasher
and the siren's wail, a man in handcuffs
gazes out at anything,
anything at all of the world...
surreal spittoon...
glow of EAT...
fresh-hit carcass ... cat ... coon...
polecat...

Suddenly lightning flashes,
path strung out across the storm,
bolt even made of hellfire
between any strange life and any strange life,
blazed
for those who shudder in their beds
hearing a siren's wail fading down
a dead-ridden highway at night...
thump ... armadillo ... thump ... dog...

4

Somebody wakes,
he's got himself a "nightcrawler"—one of those
jokes you come to in your sleep—
about girls who have "cross-bones"
and can't, some say,
be entered ... An argument now develops
on whether it is or is not possible
to circumvent the cross-bone.
"Sheee-it! Sheee-it!" the copbeater cries,
and the carthief says, "Jeee-ziz! Jeee-ziz!"
"All right boys," the pimp puts in from time to time.
"What say? Let's get a little fucking sleep."

5

One day in Ponchatoula,
watching the IC from Chicago creep
into the weeds of the Deep South, and stop,
I thought I saw three
of my kinsmen from the North
in the drinking car, boozing their way
down to New Orleans,
putting themselves across,
selling themselves,
dishing up soft soap,
plump, manicured, shit-eating, opulent, razor-sharp ...

Then the train
lurched and pushed on, carrying them off,
Yankee ... egalitarian ... grease
in the palm of their golden aspirations.

6

When I get to feeling America consists
only of billboards that smile,
I think of my friends
out there,
from Plaquemine or Point Coupee,
going from shanty to shanty
in the dust,
keeping empty
a space within them,
trudging through dust become
pollen of sunflowers under their feet.

7

The carthief's face,
oddly childish as he sleeps,
reminds me now of Jesus—a Jesus
I saw on a black funeral parlor's calendar,
blue-eyed, rosy-cheeked, milky and soft...

I remember his beautiful speech of the old days...
those prayers, funeral orations, anthems,
war songs, and—actual poems! some of them
as true as,
for example, "Wall Kill," "Terre Haute,"
"Stillwater," "Alcatraz"...
each more escapeproof,
more supersecure,
more insane than the last,
liberty, said Shelley, being
"brightest in dungeons."

The carthief moans in his sleep, his face
now like a cat's.

8

Beyond the crisscross
of bars at the tiny window
swallows dart in last light,
late-flying creatures that surpass us in plain view,
bits of blurred flesh,
wavy lines ...

Nothing's there now but a few stars
brightening
under the ice-winds of the emptiness.

Isn't it strange
that all love, all granting of respect,
has no face for its passing expressions but yours, Death?

9

I hear now
the faintest of songs, the humming
the dew makes
evaporating from the garlic leaf.

A new night
and the dew will come back,
for so many men and women
the chance to live under justice
does not ever come.

10

I remember
the ancient ex-convict who lives
in a shanty under the levee, standing
in sunlight on the dirt road.

In the green, blistered sewer,
among beer cans, weeds, plastic flowers,
a few lumps of excrement, winged
with green flies.

The dust on the road
swirls up into wing-shapes, that blow off,
the road made of dust goes down.

The air brightens as though ashes
of lightning bolts had been scattered through it.

What is it that can make a human face,
bit of secret,
lighted flesh, open the earth?

11

A girl lies with me
on the grass of the levee. Two
birds whirr overhead. We lie close, surprised
to have waked a bit early
in bodies of glory.

In its skin of light, the river
bends into view, rising
between the levees, flooding for the sky,
a hundred feet down pressing its long weight
silently into the world.

We wander slowly homeward, lost
in the history of every step.

12

I am lying face-down
by the Ten Mile River, half mud
half piss, that runs
between the Seekonk Woods
and the red mills of Pawtucket
with their thousand windows and one smokestack,
breathing the burnt air,
watching a bug break itself up,
holding to my eye a bleached catfish
skull that turned up in the grass,
inside it, in the pit of light, a cross,
hearing hornpout sounding
their horns mournfully deep inside the river.

13

Across
the dreamlit waters pushes
the flag-topped Plaquemine ferry,
midway between shore and shore
it sounds its horn, catfishes
of the Mississippi caterwaul and nose over,
heavy-skulled, into the flinty, night-smelling depths.

14

All my life, of rivers
I have heard
the longing cries, the rut-roar
of shifted wind
on gongs of beaten water:

the Ten Mile of Hornpout,
the Drac hissing in its bed of sand,
the Ruknabad scribbled over by nightingales,
the Passumpsic breaking up all down its length in spring,
the East River of Fishes, the more haunting for not having a past
        either,
the Mississippi coursing into the Gulf through the silt of all its
        days,
the snake-cracked Tangipahoa, lifting with a little rush from the
        hills and dwindling in the undernourished greenery.

15

Was there some last
fling at grace in those eddies, a swirl
of sweet scraping, out there
where an Illinois cornstalk
drifts, turning the hours,
and the grinned skull of a boy?

The burning fodder dowses down,
seeking the snagged
bodies of the water-buried,
bits
of sainfoin sopped in fire, snuffed from below

by the flesh-dark Tallahatchie,
the bone-colored Pearl.

16

I wrench a tassel of moss from a bough
to be my lightning-besom, and sweep
the mists from the way.

Ahead of me a boy is singing,

> didn't I ramble
> I rambled
> I rambled all around
> in and out the town
> I rambled
> I rambled till the butcher cut me down

He steps out of the mist,
he says his name is Henry David,
he takes my hand and leads me over the plain of crushed asphodels.

17

Who's this
at water's edge,
oar in hand, kneeling beside
his pirogue of blue stern ...
no nose left,
no hair,
no teeth,
little points of flame for eyes,
limbs tied on with knots and rags?

"Let's go," I say, a big
salty wafer of spit in my mouth.

We step in
to the threshold groan, the pressurized
bayou water squirts in
at the seams, we oar out
on water brown-green
in the patches free of scum, nothing on all sides
but a quiet, curious diet of green,
alligatorwood,
swamp gum, tupelo, liquid amber,
live oak chrisomed in air-eating moss,
cypress risen among all her failed roots.

18

Down here the air's
so thick with American radio-waves,
almost with our bare ears we can pick up
the groggy, backcountry announcers
drawling their pitches and hardsells
at old men forgotten under armies of roaches,
at babies with houseflies walking on their lips,
at men without future puking up present and past,
at recidivists sentenced deep into the hereafter,
at wineheads with only self-loathing for self-defense,
at hillbilly boys scratching their heads at the anti-sweat ads,
at...
        "Listen!" says Henry David.
"Sheee-it! Sheee-it!" a cupreous-
throated copbeater is chattering far off in the trees.

19

On the shore four shades
cry out in pain: one lashed
by red suspenders to an
ever-revolving wheel, one with
red patches on the seat of his pants
shrieking while paunchy vultures
stab at his bourbon-squirting liver,
one pushing uphill
a belly puffed up with blood money
that crashes back and crushes him,
another stuck up to his neck
in the guck he caused others to upchuck.

"Southern politicians," Henry David says.
"Yonder, in Junkie's Hollow,
you'll find Northern ones ..." I see one,
formerly mayor of a great city, withdrawing
a huge needle from his arm,
blood spurts, bits
of testicle press out through the puncture.

20

A man comes lurching
toward me with big mirrors for eyes,
"Sammich!" he cries and doubles up in laughter.
I remember him at once, from ten years ago,
in Chicago, on a Sunday
in a park on the death-scented South Side,
in the days almost before my own life had begun,
when full of strut and happiness
he came up and cried, "Sammich!"
and now he says, "A fight,
I was makin' the scene and the fuzz
did blast my fuckin' ass off." He laughs.
He is also crying. He shrinks back. "Hey,"
he calls, "thanks for that sammich
that day ... fat white bastard."

21

We come to a crowd, hornets
in their hair, worms in their feet.
"They weren't for anything or against anything,"
Henry David says, "they looked out
for themselves."
Three men trot beside us,
peddling bits of their flesh,
dishing up soft screams,
plump, manicured, shit-eating, opulent . . .

Underfoot a man
with stars on his shoulders
grapples in the slime with a large McCarthyite.
I drag the man off him and he gets up.
"In life I stood above all partisan squabbles,"
he howls,
flashes the grin
that so loved itself it sold itself to the whole world,
and at once is pulled back into the slime by a racist.

22

We come to robed
figures bunched on their knees,
meek eyes rolled up. By twitches
in their throats we gather they're alive.
"Rafel mai ameck zabi almi," they intone.

Down on all fours, like a cat
at his saucer of fresh cream, their leader,
blue-eyed, rosy-cheeked, milky and soft, laps
with big tongue at a mirror.

23

Off to one side there's a man
signing restrictive covenants with a fingernail
on a blackboard. "That one,"
says my guide, "was
well-meaning; he believed
in equality and supported good causes;
he was surprised to find out
this place is run by logicians ..."
Hearing us talk, the man half turns ...
"Come on," I tell my guide, for I know him.

24

We pass
victims of the taste for blood
who were hanged by the mob
just as the law was about to hang them,
we pass victims of justice
hanged by the mob for having obtained
stays of execution, executive pardons, fair trials,
we pass victims of prohibitions against glancing at a white woman,
who cover, as we approach, the scabs at their crotches.

Here and there stray
"unknown persons"
killed for "unknown reasons"
at the hands of "persons unknown," including
those who "just took off and caught a freight (they say)."

25

We come to a river
where thousands kneel, sucking up
its cloudy water.

"The Mystic River," Henry David says,
"the Healing Stream free to all
that flows from Calvary's Mountain ... the liquor
that makes you forget."

"And on the far shore?" "That?"
he says. "That's Camp Ground."

Behind us the police are whipping
a child who refuses to be born,
who shrieks
and scrambles for the riverbank
and stands
singing in a gospel wail,
"Oh Death, he is a little man ..."
"What's it like in Camp Ground?"

But in the mist I only hear,

> I rambled
> in and out the town
> didn't I ramble.

26

My brain rids itself of light,
at last it goes black,
slowly
slowly
a tiny cell far within it
lights up:

a man of noble face
sits on the iron bunk, wiping
a pile of knifeblades clean
in the rags of his body.
My old hero. Should I be surprised?

"Hard to wash off . . .
buffalo blood . . . Indian blood . . ." he mutters,
at each swipe singing, "*mein herz! mein herz!*"

"Why you," I ask him,
"you who, in your life, loathed our crimes?"

"Seeking love ... love
without human blood in it,
that leaps above
men and women, flesh and erections,
which was revealed to me
in a Massachusetts gravel bank in spring,
seeking love,
unable to know I only loved
mein herz! mein fucking *herz!*"

"Hey," somebody
from another cellblock shouts, "What say?
Sleep ... sleep ..."

The light goes out. In the darkness
a letter for the blind
gets put in my stunned hands.

Did I come all this way only for this, only
to feel out the world-braille of my complicity,
only to choke down this last poison wafer?

For Galway alone.
I send you my mortality.
Which leans out from itself, to spit on itself.
Which you would not touch.
All you have known.

27

On one bank
of the last river stands
a black man, on the other
a white man, on the water between
a man of no color,
body of beryl,
face of lightning,
eyes lamps of wildfire,
arms and feet polished brass.

There will come an agony upon you
beyond any
this nation has known;
and at that time thy people,
given intelligence, given imagination, given love, given . . .

Here his voice falters, he drops
to his knees, he is
falling to pieces,
no nose left,
no hair,
no teeth,
limbs dangling from prayer-knots and rags,

he sits down and waits by the grief-tree
of the last river.

Part III

Testament of the Thief

1

Under the forked
thief-shadow swinging on the breeze,
a coolie sits, resting,
shirt open,
legs spread,
head lolled to one side,
sweat-trickles,
plants,
tiny animals,
stylized all over him.

2

On good terms
with the claustrophobic pewk-worm,
the louse,
the nerve-wracked flea,

a beggar has sprawled here
all day
whether from laziness or love, while the waters

rustle in their blue grooves, and birds
ask,
      'koja? koja?'

3

"This fellow is a colonel,
the degenerate next to him is a cop,
the scarecrow in the coma is a highschool principal,
the one dyed yellow
is chief of the narcotics squad,
that meatsack smokes to bring his weight down,
the squat one
puffing tragically is a poet
broken by failure to become Minister of Finance.

"Me? I just fix
their pipes, and otherwise stab
my poor portion of the world
with skinny assbones and wait for my favorite to come,
a mean little boy
who is my most glorious punishment yet.

"Oh once
I regretted my life,
the only regret I have left,
is how much these days
they soak you for opium.

"I may be washed up,
but if you ever think of me, mull over
this proverb, will you? *If
the cat had wings
he would gobble up every bird in the sky.*"

4

The wild rose dies,
the hollyhock falls before finishing its blossoming,
the poppy does not come back,
the moth preens herself by stages
for her carnal moment.

And yet a rose
has tossed the corpse its perfume.
That that bloated snout can catch it proves
the body, too,
has its origins in paradise.

5

A breeze from the bazaar,
lotus,
wild olive,
gum tragacanth,
indigo, musk,
burnt seed of wild rue,
gillyflower...

The poor huddle at
pushcarts of fire, eating
boiled beets,
gut,
tongue,
testicle,
cheeks, forehead, little feet.

Down this street the thief
would pick his way, in his pajamas.
After a meal he would sprawl
on just this spot, letting earth
draw down his bones upon her.

Stop a moment on his bones' dents,
stand without moving, listen
to the ordinary people
as they pass. They do not sing
of what is gone or to come, they sing
of the old testaments of their lives,
the little meals,
the airs,
the streets of our time.

6

"*Item,* to the opium master
dying from too much paradise: this round nose,
in working disorder,
that tracks down
the fumes of the real.

"*Item,* to the beggar
dumped on blue stone, gasping
as, one after one, the friends
of his youth hallucinate his sleep:
this set of bones, their
iron faithfulness to loss.

"*Item*, to the navvy
who trudges over the earth
bearing earth on his backbones,
whose skeleton at the last will howl
for its dust just like any other:
this ultimate ruckus on the groan-meat."

7

Item, to the pewk-worm
who lives all his life inside flesh,
sleaching along through fat or lean,
skinny or soft, gnawing himself
 a peephole when lost, in buttock or cheek,
whom you can drag out of you
only by winding him up on a matchstick
a quarter turn a day for the rest of your days:
these crawl-maps of my innards.

The Porcupine

1

Fatted
on herbs, swollen on crabapples,
puffed up on bast and phloem, ballooned
on willow flowers, poplar catkins, first
leafs of aspen and larch,
the porcupine
drags and bounces his last meal through ice,
mud, roses and goldenrod, into the stubbly high fields.

2

In character
he resembles us in seven ways:
he puts his mark on outhouses,
he alchemizes by moonlight,
he shits on the run,
he uses his tail for climbing,
he chuckles softly to himself when scared,
he's overcrowded if there's more than one of him per five acres,
his eyes have their own inner redness.

3

Digger of
goings across floors, of hesitations

at thresholds, of
handprints of dread
at doorpost or window jamb, he would
gouge the world
empty of us, hack and crater
it
until it is nothing, if that
could rid it of all our sweat and pathos.

Adorer of ax
handles aflow with grain, of arms
of Morris chairs, of hand
crafted objects
steeped in the juice of fingertips,
of surfaces wetted down
with fist grease or elbow oil,
of clothespins that have
grabbed our body rags by underarm and crotch...

Unimpressed—bored—
by the whirl of the stars, by *these*
he's astonished, ultra-
Rilkean angel!

for whom the true
portion of the sweetness of earth
is one of those bottom-heavy, glittering, saccadic
bits
of salt water that splash down
the haunted ravines of a human face.

4

A farmer shot a porcupine three times
as it dozed on a tree limb. On
the way down it tore open its belly
on a broken
branch, hooked its gut,
and went on falling. On the ground
it sprang to its feet
and paying out gut heaved
and spartled through a hundred feet of goldenrod
before
the abrupt emptiness.

5

The Avesta
puts porcupine killers
into hell for nine generations, sentencing them
to gnaw out
each other's hearts for the
salts of desire.

I roll
this way and that in the great bed, under
the quilt
that mimics this country of broken farms and woods,
the fatty sheath of the man
melting off,
the self-stabbing coil
of bristles reversing, blossoming outward—

a red-eyed, hard-toothed, arrow-stuck urchin
tossing up mattress feathers,
pricking the
woman beside me until she cries.

6

In my time I have
crouched, quills erected,
Saint
Sebastian of the
scared heart, and been
beat dead with a locust club
on the bare snout.
And fallen from high places
I have fled, have
jogged
over fields of goldenrod,
terrified, seeking home,
and among flowers
I have come to myself empty, the rope
strung out behind me
in the fall sun
suddenly glorified with all my blood.

7

And tonight I think I prowl broken
skulled or vacant as a
sucked egg in the wintry meadow, softly chuckling, blank

template of myself, dragging
a starved belly through the lichflowered acres,
where burdock looses its arks of seed
and thistle holds up its lost blooms
and rosebushes in the wind scrape their dead limbs
for the forced-fire
of roses.

The Bear

1

In late winter
I sometimes glimpse bits of steam
coming up from
some fault in the old snow
and bend close and see it is lung-colored
and put down my nose
and know
the chilly, enduring odor of bear.

2

I take a wolf's rib and whittle
it sharp at both ends
and coil it up
and freeze it in blubber and place it out
on the fairway of the bears.

And when it has vanished
I move out on the bear tracks,
roaming in circles
until I come to the first, tentative, dark
splash on the earth.

And I set out
running, following the splashes
of blood wandering over the world.

At the cut, gashed resting places
I stop and rest,
at the crawl-marks
where he lay out on his belly
to overpass some stretch of bauchy ice
I lie out
dragging myself forward with bear-knives in my fists.

3

On the third day I begin to starve,
at nightfall I bend down as I knew I would
at a turd sopped in blood,
and hesitate, and pick it up,
and thrust it in my mouth, and gnash it down,
and rise
and go on running.

4

On the seventh day,
living by now on bear blood alone,
I can see his upturned carcass far out ahead, a scraggled,
steamy hulk,
the heavy fur riffling in the wind.

I come up to him
and stare at the narrow-spaced, petty eyes,
the dismayed
face laid back on the shoulder, the nostrils

flared, catching
perhaps the first taint of me as he
died.

I hack
a ravine in his thigh, and eat and drink,
and tear him down his whole length
and open him and climb in
and close him up after me, against the wind,
and sleep.

5

And dream
of lumbering flatfooted
over the tundra,
stabbed twice from within,
splattering a trail behind me,
splattering it out no matter which way I lurch,
no matter which parabola of bear-transcendence,
which dance of solitude I attempt,
which gravity-clutched leap,
which trudge, which groan.

6

Until one day I totter and fall—
fall on this
stomach that has tried so hard to keep up,
to digest the blood as it leaked in,

to break up
and digest the bone itself: and now the breeze
blows over me, blows off
the hideous belches of ill-digested bear blood
and rotted stomach
and the ordinary, wretched odor of bear,

blows across
my sore, lolled tongue a song
or screech, until I think I must rise up
and dance. And I lie still.

7

I awaken I think. Marshlights
reappear, geese
come trailing again up the flyway.
In her ravine under old snow the dam-bear
lies, licking
lumps of smeared fur
and drizzly eyes into shapes
with her tongue. And one
hairy-soled trudge stuck out before me,
the next groaned out,
the next,
the next,
the rest of my days I spend
wandering: wondering
what, anyway,
was that sticky infusion, that rank flavor of blood, that poetry, by
    which I lived?

Mortal Acts, Mortal Words

to Demetrio Delgado de Torres
tu valiente alegría

PART I

Fergus Falling

He climbed to the top
of one of those million white pines
set out across the emptying pastures
of the fifties—some program to enrich the rich
and rebuke the forefathers
who cleared it all once with ox and axe—
climbed to the top, probably to get out
of the shadow
not of those forefathers but of this father,
and saw for the first time,
down in its valley, Bruce Pond, giving off
its little steam in the afternoon,

pond where Clarence Akley came on Sunday mornings to cut
    down the cedars around the shore, I'd sometimes hear the
    slow spondees of his work, he's gone,
where Milton Norway came up behind me while I was fishing and
    stood awhile before I knew he was there, he's the one who put
    the cedar shingles on the house, some have curled or split, a
    few have blown off, he's gone,
where Gus Newland logged in the cold snap of '58, the only man
    willing to go into those woods that never got warmer than ten
    below, he's gone,
pond where two wards of the state wandered on Halloween, the
    National Guard searched for them in November, in vain, the
    next fall a hunter found their skeletons huddled together, in
    vain, they're gone,
pond where an old fisherman in a rowboat sits, drowning hooked
    worms, when he goes he's replaced and he's never gone,

and when Fergus
saw the pond for the first time
in the clear evening, saw its oldness down there
in its old place in the valley, he became heavier suddenly
in his bones
the way fledglings do just before they fly,
and the soft pine cracked...

I would not have heard his cry
if my electric saw had been working,
its carbide teeth speeding through the bland spruce of our time, or
    scorching
black arcs into some scavenged hemlock plank,
like dark circles under eyes
when the brain thinks too close to the skin,
but I was sawing by hand, and I heard that cry
as though he were attacked; we ran out,
when we bent over him he said, "Galway, Inés, I saw a pond!"
His face went gray, his eyes fluttered closed a frightening moment.

Yes—a pond
that lets off its mist
on clear afternoons of August, in that valley
to which many have come, for their reasons,
from which many have gone, a few for their reasons, most not,
where even now an old fisherman only the pinetops can see
sits in the dry gray wood of his rowboat, waiting for pickerel.

After Making Love We Hear Footsteps

For I can snore like a bullhorn
or play loud music
or sit up talking with any reasonably sober Irishman
and Fergus will only sink deeper
into his dreamless sleep, which goes by all in one flash,
but let there be that heavy breathing
or a stifled come-cry anywhere in the house
and he will wrench himself awake
and make for it on the run—as now, we lie together,
after making love, quiet, touching along the length of our bodies,
familiar touch of the long-married,
and he appears—in his baseball pajamas, it happens,
the neck opening so small he has to screw them on—
and flops down between us and hugs us and snuggles himself to
     sleep,
his face gleaming with satisfaction at being this very child.

In the half darkness we look at each other
and smile
and touch arms across this little, startlingly muscled body—
this one whom habit of memory propels to the ground of his
     making,
sleeper only the mortal sounds can sing awake,
this blessing love gives again into our arms.

Angling, a Day

Though day is just breaking
when we fling two nightcrawlers
bunched on a hook as far out
as we can into Crystal Lake so leaden
no living thing could possibly swim through it
and let them lie on the bottom, under
the layer of water and, on top of it,
the layer of mist in which the doubled sun
soon appears and before long the doubled
mountains; though we drag Lake Parker
with fishing apparatus of several sorts,
catching a few yellow perch which we keep
just to have caught *something;* though
we comb with fine, and also coarse,
toothed hooks Shirley's Pond stocked
with trout famous for swallowing
any sharpened wire no matter
how inexpertly disguised as a worm;
though we fish the pools thick with fish
Bill Allen has divined by dip of bamboo
during all those misspent days trout-witching
Miller Run; though we cast some hours
away at the Lamoille, at the bend
behind Eastern Magnesia Talc Company's
Mill No. 4, which Hayden Carruth
says his friend John Engles says
is the best fishing around ("hernia bend,"

Engels calls it, I believe on account of the weight
of fish you haul out of there); and though we
fish the Salmon Hole of the Winooski
in which twenty-inch walleyes moil,
we and a dozen others who keep faith
with earth by the thinness of that string
tying each person to the river at twilight,
casting and, as we reel in, twitching the rod,
our bodies curvetting in that curious motion
by which people giving fish motions to lures
wiggle themselves like fish, until Fergus' jig,
catching a rock as he reels in,
houdinies out of its knot, and the man
fishing next to us, Ralph, reeling
somewhat himself due to an afternoon of much ale,
lends us one of his, and with shaking hands
ties a stout knot between line and jig,
while a fellow from downcountry
goes on about how to free a snagged line
by sliding a spark plug down it—
"Well," Ralph says a couple of times,
"I sure never heard of that one,"
though sure enough, a few minutes later,
when Ralph's own line gets snagged,
he takes the fellow up on the idea,
borrows the man's spark plug, taps
the gap closed over the line as directed,
and lets her slide, wiggling
vigorously as the plug disappears
into the water, and instantly loses it

and the jig both, and says, "Nope,
I sure never heard of that one"—
though, in brief, we have crossed the entire state
up at its thick end, and fished with hope
all the above-mentioned fishing spots
from before first light to after nightfall
and now will just be able to make it
to Essex Junction in time
to wait the several hours that must pass
before the train arrives in reality,
we have caught nothing—not counting,
of course, the three yellow perch Fergus
gave away earlier in the day to Bill and Anne
Allen's cat Monsoon, who is mostly dead
along her left side though OK on her right,
the side she was no doubt lying on the night
last winter when, literally, she half froze to death—
and wondering if Fergus, who's so tired
he now gets to his feet only to cast
and at once sits back down, might be thoroughly
defeated, and his noble passion for fishing
broken, I ask him how he feels:
"I'm disappointed," he says, "but not discouraged.
I'm not saying I'm a fisherman, but fishermen know
there are days when you don't catch anything."

Saint Francis and the Sow

The bud
stands for all things,
even for those things that don't flower,
for everything flowers, from within, of self-blessing;
though sometimes it is necessary
to reteach a thing its loveliness,
to put a hand on its brow
of the flower
and retell it in words and in touch
it is lovely
until it flowers again from within, of self-blessing;
as Saint Francis
put his hand on the creased forehead
of the sow, and told her in words and in touch
blessings of earth on the sow, and the sow
began remembering all down her thick length,
from the earthen snout all the way
through the fodder and slops to the spiritual curl of the tail,
from the hard spininess spiked out from the spine
down through the great broken heart
to the sheer blue milken dreaminess spurting and shuddering
from the fourteen teats into the fourteen mouths sucking and
     blowing beneath them:
the long, perfect loveliness of sow.

The Choir

Little beings with hair blooming
so differently on skulls of odd sizes
and eyes serious and jaws
firm from singing in Gilead,
and mouths gaping, "Ah!" for God
and "O!" for alphabets short on O's,
they stand in rows, each suspended
from that fishing line
hooked at the breastbone, ready to be hauled upward.

Everyone while singing is beautiful.
Even the gloomiest music
requires utter happiness to sing:
eyes, nostrils, mouth must delight each other in quintal harmony
to sing Joy or Death well.

Two Set Out on Their Journey

We sit side by side,
brother and sister, and read
the book of what will be, while a breeze
blows the pages over—
desolate odd, cheerful even,
and otherwise. When we come
to our own story, the happy beginning,
the ending we don't know yet,
the ten thousand acts
encumbering the days between,
we will read every page of it.
If an ancestor has pressed
a love-flower for us, it will lie hidden
between pages of the slow going,
where only those who adore the story
ever read. When the time comes
to shut the book and set out,
we will take childhood's laughter
as far as we can into the days to come,
until another laughter sounds back
from the place where our next bodies
will have risen and will be telling
tales of what seemed deadly serious once,
offering to us oldening wayfarers
the light heart, now made of time
and sorrow, that we started with.

Brother of My Heart

for Etheridge Knight

Brother of my heart,
isn't it true there's only one
walking into the light, one,
before the light
flashes out and this bravest knight
crashes his black bones into the earth?

You may not return
with your cried-out face
laughing; those who
die by the desire to die
may love their way back,
but maybe as grubs who latch
on to the first sorrow and lie there.

And so just as you are,
sing, even if you cry; the bravery
of the singing turns it into the true song; soul brother
in heaven, on earth
broken heart brother, sing
in this place that loses its brothers,
this emptiness the singing sometimes almost fills.

Fisherman

for Allen Planz

Solitary man, standing
on the Atlantic, high up on the floodtide
under the moon, hauling at nets
that shudder sideways under the mutilated darkness:
the one you hugged and slept with so often,
who hugged you and slept with you so often,
who has gone away now
into the imaginary moonlight of the greater world,
perhaps looks back at where you stand abandoned
on the floodtide, hauling at nets
and dragging from the darkness
anything, and reaches back
as if to touch you
and speak to you
from that other relation to which she suddenly acquiesced
    dumbfounded,
but finds she can only sing to you
in the sea-birds and breeze you truly hear but imagine you're
    remembering.

I don't know how you loved
or what marriage was and wasn't between you—
not even close friends understand very much of that—
but I know ordinary life was hard
and worry joined your brains' faces in pure, baffled lines,
and therefore some part of you will have gone
with her, imprinted now

into that world that she alone doesn't fear
and that now you have to that degree also ceased fearing,
and waits there to recognize you into it
after you've lived, lived past the sorrows,
if that happens, after all the time in the world.

Wait

Wait, for now.
Distrust everything if you have to.
But trust the hours. Haven't they
carried you everywhere, up to now?
Personal events will become interesting again.
Hair will become interesting.
Pain will become interesting.
Buds that open out of season will become interesting.
Second-hand gloves will become lovely again;
their memories are what give them
the need for other hands. The desolation
of lovers is the same: that enormous emptiness
carved out of such tiny beings as we are
asks to be filled; the need
for the new love *is* faithfulness to the old.

Wait.
Don't go too early.
You're tired. But everyone's tired.
But no one is tired enough.
Only wait a little and listen:
music of hair,
music of pain,
music of looms weaving our loves again.
Be there to hear it, it will be the only time,
most of all to hear your whole existence,
rehearsed by the sorrows, play itself into total exhaustion.

PART II

Daybreak

On the tidal mud, just before sunset,
dozens of starfishes
were creeping. It was
as though the mud were a sky
and enormous, imperfect stars
moved across it as slowly
as the actual stars cross heaven.
All at once they stopped,
and as if they had simply
increased their receptivity
to gravity, they sank down
into the mud, faded down
into it and lay still, and by the time
pink of sunset broke across them
they were as invisible
as the true stars at daybreak.

The Gray Heron

It held its head still
while its body and green
legs wobbled in wide arcs
from side to side. When
it stalked out of sight,
I went after it, but all
I could find where I was
expecting to see the bird
was a three-foot-long lizard
in ill-fitting skin
and with linear mouth
expressive of the even temper
of the mineral kingdom.
It stopped and tilted its head,
which was much like
a fieldstone with an eye
in it, which was watching me
to see if I would go
or change into something else.

In the Bamboo Hut

The washerwomen would throw dresses,
shirts, pants, into the green water,
beat them, wring them out,
arrange them empty in our shapes
on stones, murmuring, laughing,
sometimes a voice more forlorn
would rise above the others, a singing
like the aftersinging, those nights
when we would wail as one under
the sign of the salamander, motionless,
attentive, on the wall above our bed.

Lava

(The Hawaiian words—*pahoehoe, aa,* and *heiau*—are
pronounced pä•hō•ä•hō•ä; ä•ä; and hā•ē•ow.)

I want to be pahoehoe,
swirled, gracefully lined,
folded, frozen where it flowed,
a clear brazened surface
one can cross barefooted,
it's true; but even more,
I want to be aa,
a mass of rubble still
tumbling after it has stopped—
which a person without shoes
has to do deep knee-bends across,
groaning "aaaah! aaaah!"—
and be heaped into a heiau
in sea-spray on an empty coast,
and know in all my joints
the soft, velcroish clasp
of aa hanging on to aa.

When I approach the dismal shore
made I know of pahoehoe,
which is just hoi polloi of the slopes,
I don't want to call "ahoy! ahoy!"
and sail meekly in. No,
I want to turn and look back
at that glittering, black aa
where we loved in the moon,

and all our atoms broke and lived,
where even now two kneecaps gasp
"ah! ah!" to a heiau's stone floor,
to which the floor replies
"aaaaaah, aaaaaah," in commiseration
with bones that find the way very long.

Blackberry Eating

I love to go out in late September
among the fat, overripe, icy, black blackberries
to eat blackberries for breakfast,
the stalks very prickly, a penalty
they earn for knowing the black art
of blackberry making; and as I stand among them
lifting the stalks to my mouth, the ripest berries
fall almost unbidden to my tongue,
as words sometimes do, certain peculiar words
like *strengths* or *squinched* or *broughamed*,
many-lettered, one-syllabled lumps,
which I squeeze, squinch open, and splurge well
in the silent, startled, icy, black language
of blackberry eating in late September.

Kissing the Toad

Somewhere this dusk
a girl puckers her mouth
and considers kissing
the toad a boy has plucked
from the cornfield and hands
her with both hands,
rough and lichenous
but for the immense ivory belly,
like those old fat cats
sprawled on Mediterranean beaches,
with popped eyes, it watches
the girl who might kiss it,
pisses, quakes, tries
to make its smile wider:
to love on, oh yes, to love on.

Crying

Crying only a little bit
is no use. You must cry
until your pillow is soaked.
Then you can get up and laugh.
Then you can jump in the shower
and splash-splash-splash!
Then you can throw open your window
and, "Ha ha! ha ha!"
And if people say, "Hey,
what's going on up there?"
"Ha ha!" sing back, "Happiness
was hiding in the last tear!
I wept it! Ha ha!"

Les Invalides

At dusk by Les Invalides
a few old men play at boules,
holding the crouch
long after the toss, listening for the clack
of steel on steel, strolling over and studying the ground.

At boules, it is the creaking grace, the slow amble, the stillness,
the dusk deepening,
a plane tree casting loose a few leaves,
shadows lying behind the undistracted eyes.

It is empty cots lined up
in the darkness of rooms where the last true men
listen each dusk
for the high, thin clack
sounding from the home village very far away.

On the Tennis Court at Night

We step out on the green rectangle
in moonlight. The lines glow,
which for many have been the only lines
of justice. We remember
the thousand erased trajectories
of that close-contested last set —
blur of volleys, soft arcs of drop shots,
huge ingrown loops of lobs with topspin
that went running away, crosscourts recrossing
down to each sweet (and in exact proportion, bitter)
✪ in Talbert and Old's *The Game of Doubles in Tennis*.
The breeze has carried them off but we still hear
the mutters, the doublefaulter's groans,
cries of "Deuce!" or "Love two!",
squeak of tennis shoes, grunt of overreaching,
all dozen extant tennis quips — "Just out!"
or, "About right for you?" or, "Want to change partners?" —
and *baaah* of sheep translated very occasionally
into *thonk* of well-hit ball, among the pure
right angles and unhesitating lines
of this arena where every man grows old
pursuing that repertoire of perfect shots,
darkness already in his strokes,
even in death cramps squeezing a tennis ball
for forearm strength, to the disgust of the night nurse,
and smiling; and a few hours later found dead —
the smile still in place but the ice bag

that had been left cooling the brow now
icing the right elbow—causing
all the bright trophies to slip permanently out of reach,
except for the thick-bottomed young man
about to doublefault in soft metal on the windowsill:
"Runner-Up Men's Class B Consolation Doubles
St. Johnsbury Kiwanis Tennis Tournament 1969."

Clouds come over the moon;
the lines go out. November last year
in Lyndonville: it is getting dark,
snow starts falling, Zander Rubin wobble-twists
his worst serve out of the black woods behind him,
Tommy Glines lobs into a gust of snow,
Don Bredes smashes at where in theory the ball
could be coming down, the snow blows
and swirls about our legs, darkness flows
across a disappearing patch of green-painted asphalt
in the north country, where four souls,
half-volleying, poaching, missing, grunting,
begging mercy of their bones, hold their ground,
as winter comes on, all the winters to come.

PART III

The Sadness of Brothers

1

He comes to me like a mouth
speaking from under several inches of water.
I can no longer understand what he is saying.
He has become one
who never belonged among us, someone
it is useless to think about or remember.

But this morning, I don't know why,
twenty-one years too late,
I imagine him back: his beauty
of feature somewhat wastreled down
to wattles and thick chin, his eyes
ratty, liver-lighted, he stands
in the doorway and we face each other,
each of us knowing the lost brother.

2

There was a photograph
of a tractor ploughing a field, the ploughman
twisted in his iron seat
looking behind him at the turned-up earth, among
the photographs and drawings he had hoarded up
of all the aircraft in the sky, Heinkel HE70s, Dewoitine D333
     "Antares," Loire-et-Olivier H24-2,

especially the fighting aircraft, Gloster Gauntlet, Fairey Battle I,
    Vickers Vildebeest Mark VII,
each shown crookedly
climbing an empty sky
the killer's blue of his eyes,
into which all his youth he knew
he would fly. Twelve years after
the war and the end of flying
he raced his big car
through the desert night, under
the Dipper that moved
like a great windshield wiper
squeegee-ing existence
clean of its damaged dream life
leaving only old goods, few possessions,
matter which ceased to matter, among the detritus,
these photographs of airplanes, and showing off
its gravitational allegiance
the tractor, and in its iron
seat the farmer, half-turned, watching
the earth flattening away
behind him into nowhere.

3

In this brother
I remember back is the father
I had so often seen in him: the serene-
seeming, sea-going gait which took him
down Oswald Street in dark of each morning

and up Oswald Street in dark of each night,
that small, well-wandered Scotsman
who appears now in memory's memory,
in light of last days, jiggling
his knees as he used to do—
get out of here, I knew
they were telling him, *get out of here, Scotty*—
control he couldn't control
thwarting his desires down
into knees which could only jiggle
the one bit of perhaps useful advice
this man stuck in his ending-earth
of Pawtucket, Rhode Island, ever received.

4

I think he's going to ask
for beer for breakfast, sooner
or later he'll start making obnoxious
remarks about race or sex
or criticize our loose ways
of raising children, while his eyes
grow more slick, his heart more pure,
this boy who at sixteen
would slip out at night, blackjack
in pocket, .22 pistol in armpit holster,
to make out with rich men's wives
at the Narragansett Track, now vanished
from its site on the even more vanished
What Cheer Airport, where a Waco biplane

flew up for a joyride in 1931
with him waving from the rear cockpit.

5

But no, that's fear's reading. In the doorway,
in the frailty of large,
fifty-odd-year-old bodies
of brothers, we stand—
in this vision that came to me today
of a man twenty-one years strange to me,
tired, vulnerable, half the world old,
with sore, well or badly spent, but spent,
hearts—facing each other, friends with reality,
knowing the ordinary sadness of brothers.

Goodbye

1

My mother, poor woman, lies tonight
in her last bed. It's snowing, for her, in her darkness.
I swallow down the goodbyes I won't ever get to use,
tasteless, with wretched mouth-water;
whatever we are, she and I, we're nearly cured.

The night years ago when I walked away
from that final class of junior high school students
in Pittsburgh, the youngest of them chased
after me down the dark street. "Goodbye!" she called,
snow swirling across her face, tears shining.

2

Tears have a history of falling. Gravity
has taught them a topographical understanding
of the human face. At each last embrace
the snow brings down its ragged curtain.
The mind shreds the present, once the past is over.

In the Derry graveyard where only her longings sleep
and armfuls of flowers go out in the drizzle,
the bodies not yet risen must lie nearly forever.
"Sprouting good Irish grass," the graveskeeper blarneys,
he can't help it, "a sprig of shamrock, if they were young."

3

In Pittsburgh tonight, those who were young
will be less young, those who were old, more old, or likely
no more; and the street where Syllest,
fleetest of my darlings, caught up with me
and hugged me and said goodbye will be empty. Well,

one day the streets all over the world will be empty—
already in heaven the golden cobblestones have fallen still—
everyone's arms will be empty, everyone's mouth, the Derry earth.
It is written in our hearts, the emptiness is all.
That is how we have learned, the embrace is all.

Looking at Your Face

Looking at your face
now you have become ready to die
is like kneeling at an old gravestone
on an afternoon without sun, trying to read
the white chiselings of the poem
in the white stone.

The Last Hiding Places of Snow

The burnt tongue
fluttered, "I'm dying..."
and then, "Why did ...? Why...?"
What earthly knowledge did she need
just then, when
the tongue failed
or began speaking in another direction?

Only the struggle for breath
remained: groans made
of all the goodbyes ever spoken
all turned meaningless; surplus world sucked back
into a body laboring to live
as far as it could into death; and past it, if it must.

There is a place in the woods
where one can hear
such sounds: sighs, groans
seeming to come
from the purplish murk of spruce boughs at dusk,
from the glimmer-at-night of white birches,
from the last hiding places of snow,

wind,
that's all, blowing
across obstructions: every stump
speaks,
spruce needles play out of it
the sorrows cried into it somewhere else.

Passing the place, I've
imagined I heard
my old mother thinking out loud her
feelings toward me, over those many miles
from where her bones lie,
five years
in earth now, with my father's thirty-years' bones.

I used to feel
anointed by what I thought was her love, its light
seeming then like sunlight
falling through broken panes
onto the floor
of a deserted house: we may go, it remains,
telling of goodness of being, of permanence.

So lighted I imagined
I could wander anywhere,
among any foulnesses, any contagions,
I could climb through the entire empty world
and find my way back and learn again to be happy.

But when I stopped and listened,
all that may once have been speech
or groans had been shredded down to a hiss
from being blown through this valley of needles.

   2

I was not at her bedside
that final day, I did not grant her ancient,
huge-knuckled hand
its last wish, I did not let it
let go of the son's hand gradually—and so
hand her, with some steadiness, into the future.

Instead, old age took her
by force, though with the aid
of her old, broken attachments
which had broken
only on this side of death
but kept intact on the other.

I would know myself lucky if my own children
could be at my deathbed, to take
my hand in theirs and with theirs
bless me momentarily back into the world,
with smoothness pressed into roughness,
with folding-light fresh runner hands to runner of wasted breath,
with mortal touch whose mercy two bundled-up figures greeting
    on a freezing morning, each extending the ribboned end of
    an arm and entwining these, squeeze back and forth before
    walking on,

with memories these hands keep, of strolling down Bethune Street
    in spring, a little creature hanging from each arm by a hand
    that can do no more than press its tiny thumb into the soft
    beneath my thumb.

But for my own mother I was not there...
and at the gates of the world, between
holy ground
and ground of almost all its holiness gone, I loiter
in stupid fantasies I can live that day again.

Why did you come so late?
Why will you go too early?

I know there are regrets
we can never be rid of,
that fade but never leave:
permanent remorse. Knowing this, I know also
I am to draw from that surplus stored up
of tenderness that was hers by right,
which possibly no one ever gave her,
and give it away, freely.

   3

A child, a little girl,
in violet hat, blue scarf, green sweater, yellow skirt, orange socks,
    red boots,
on a rope swings, swings
in sunlight

over a garden in Ireland, backfalls,
backrises,
forthsinks,
forthsoars, her charmed life holding its breath
innocent of groans, beyond any
future, far past the past: into a pure present.

Now she wears rhythmically into the air of morning
the rainbow's curve, but upside down
so that the angels might see
beloved dross promising heaven:
no matter what fire we invent to destroy us
ours will have been the brightest world ever existing.

Every so often, when I look
at the dark sky, I know she remains
among the old endless blue lightedness
of stars; or finding myself out in a field
in November, when a strange
starry perhaps first snowfall blows
down across the darkening air, lightly,
I know she is there, where snow
falls flakes down fragile softly
falling until I can't see the earth
any longer, only its shrouded shapes.

Even now, when I wake
in some room far from everyone,
sometimes the darkness lightens a little,
and then, because of nothing,

in spite of nothing,
in an imaginary daybreak, I see her,
and for that moment I am still her son
and in the holy land, and twice in the holy land,
remembered within her, and remembered in the memory
her old body slowly executes into the earth.

52 Oswald Street

for my sisters Wendy and Jill

Then, when the full moonlight
would touch our blanketed bodies,
we liked to think it filled
us with actual bright matter
drifted down from the regions
of the moon, so that when we woke
we would be changed. Now,
wherever we are on earth,
in loneliness, or loneliness-
easing arms, we three
who have survived the lives
and deaths in the old house
on Oswald Street can almost
feel that full moonlight again,
as someone might hear the slow-
given sighs of post-coital bliss
the lover who took off could be
breathing this minute in someone
else's arms, and taste
the lost fullness and know how
far our hearts have fallen, how
our feelings too long attuned
to having don't bear up,
and how for us it turns out
three gravesides were too many
to stand at, or turn from,
that most mired of pivotings,

and our mouths fill with three
names that can't find their meanings,
theirs, and before we know it, also
ours, and we pull up more tightly
around us the coverings of
full moonlight that fall down
now from unrepeatable life
on bodies of mother and father
and three children, and a fourth,
sleeping, quite long ago.

PART IV

The Rainbow

The rainbow appears above us
for its minute, then vanishes, as though
we had wished it, making us
turn more carefully to what we can
touch, things and creatures
we know we haven't dreamed: flutings
on a match stick, the blurry
warmth a match gives back
to thumb and forefinger
when we hold it to the spewing
gas, for instance, or
the pelvic bones of a woman
lying on her back, which rise
on either side of the crater
we floated in, in the first life,
that last time we knew
more of happiness than of time,
before the world-ending inkling
of what pain would be for all
of our natural going—a blow
so well-struck space
simply breaks—befell us.
Then we fell, scanning about,
the cleverest of us, for a lover
to cling to, and howling
howls of the damned so fierce
they put terrified grooves

permanently into the throat,
until the day the carcass
has swirled its defeated desire
toward those invisible fires,
the other, unfulfilled galaxies,
to win them over, too, into time and ruin.

The Apple

The brain
cringes around the worst
that it knows; just as the apple
must have done, around the poison
said to have poisoned those two
into the joy
that watches itself go away.

No one easily
survives love; neither the love
one has, nor the love
one has not; they break down
in the red smoke blown up
of the day when all love will have gone on.

A little sadness,
a little more self-cruelty,
a little more uselessness
added to our world.
These won't last.
What will last is that
no one will know
to let go, everyone will need
the one he or she doesn't know
all the way to the day we become
moonstones, broken open
under the moon, only an
icy brightness remembering inside us.

Memory of Wilmington

Thirty-some years ago, hitchhiking
north on Route 1, I stopped for the night
at Wilmington, Delaware, one of those American cities
that start falling apart before they ever get finished.
I met, I remember, an ancient hobo—I almost remember
his name—at the ferry—now dead,
of course, him,
and also the ferry—
in great-brimmed hat, coat to his knees,
pants dragging the ground, semi-zootish rig
plucked off various clotheslines.

He taught me how to grab a hen
so the dogs won't hear: come up on it
from behind, swoop down and seize it
and whirl it up, all in one motion
breaking the neck, and also twisting
silent any cry
of alarm it might start to utter.

It doesn't matter.

It doesn't matter
that we ill-roasted our hen over brushwood
or that with the squeamishness
of the young I dismouthed the rawest of it
into the black waters of Delaware Bay.

After he ate, the old hobo
—*Amos!* yes, that's it!—old Amos
rasped out a song or two, his voice
creaking more and more slowly,
like a music box when time slows itself down inside it.
I sat in the last light and listened, among rocks,
tin cans, feathers, ashes, old stars.

The next day when I sailed north
on the ferry the sun was shining.
From the decaying landing Amos waved.
I was fifteen, I think. Wilmington then
was far along on its way to becoming a city
and equally advanced on its way back to dust.

The Still Time

I know there is still time—
time for the hands
to open,
to be filled
by those failed harvests,
the imagined bread of the days of not having.

I remember those summer nights
when I was young and empty,
when I lay through the darkness
wanting, wanting,
knowing
I would have nothing of anything I wanted—
that total craving
that can hollow a heart out irreversibly.

So it surprises me now to hear
the steps of my life following me—
so much of it gone
it returns, everything that drove me crazy
comes back, as if to modify the misery
of each step it took me into the world;
as though a prayer had ended
and the changed
air between the palms went free
to become that inexplicable
glittering we see on ordinary things.

And the voices,
which once made broken-off, parrot-incoherences,
speak again, this time
speaking on the palatum cordis,
saying there is time, still time
for those who can groan to sing,
for those who can sing to be healed.

There Are Things I Tell to No One

1

There are things I tell to no one.
Those close to me might think
I was depressed, and try to comfort me.
At such times I go off alone, in silence, as if listening for God.

2

I say "God"; I believe,
rather, in a music of grace
that we hear, sometimes, playing
from the other side of happiness.
When we hear it and it flows
through our bodies, it lets us live
these days intensified by their vanity
worshipping, as the other animals do,
who live and die in the spirit
of the end, that backward-spreading
brightness. It speaks in notes struck
or caressed or blown or plucked
off our own bodies: *remember*
existence already remembers
the flush upon it you will have been,
you who have reached out ahead
and touched the dust we become.

3

Just as the supreme cry
of joy also has a ghastliness to it,
as though it touched forward
into the chaos where we break apart,
so the death-groan, though sounding
from another direction, carries us back
to our first world, where we see
a grandmother sitting only yesterday
oddly fearless on the tidy porch, her little boned body drowsing
    almost unobserved into the agreement to die.

4

Brothers and sisters;
lovers and children;
great mothers and grand fathers
whose love-times have been chiseled
by now into stone; great
grand fœtuses spelling
the past into the flesh's waters:
can you bless, or not curse,
everything that struggles to stay alive
on this planet of struggles?

Then the last cry in the throat
or only imagined into it
by its threads too wasted to make sound,
will disappear into the music
that carries our time on earth

away, on the catafalque
of bones marrowed with god's-flesh,
thighs bruised by the blue flower,
pelvis that makes angels shiver to know down here we make love
    with our bones,
I want to live forever. But when I hear
through the walls grace-notes blown
out of the wormed-out bones,
music that their memory of blood
plucks from the straitened arteries,
music that lovers caressed from each other
in the holy days of their vanity,
that the two hearts drummed
out of their ribs together,
the hearts that know everything (and even
the little knowledge they can leave
stays, to be the light of this house),
then it is not so difficult
to go out and turn and face
the spaces that gather into one
sound the waves of spent existence
that flow toward, and toward, and on which we flow
and grow drowsy and become fearless again.

Pont Neuf at Nightfall

Just now a sprinkling
of rain begins. It brings with it
an impression of more lasting existence —
brings it by removal, by the swiftness
of each drop's drying from the stone.
When stone becomes wet, that's
when desolation comes into the world.
We can't grasp our full debt to those
who heaped up stones into palaces,
arches, spires, into a grace
which, being behind us, is beyond us.
But we pay them some envy, we imagine
a reality filled almost completely
with what is, without room
for longing backward; and also
the knowledge that happiness exists
even if sometimes out of reach.
A girl walks by, a presence
in someone's anticipation, she is
clasping flowers, trailing
their odor and their memory
of her into a past so brief
it follows close behind.
A light comes on very dim in a hotel
window, a glint of what once was
the light of the world. In a tiny room
overlooking a bridge and a dark river,

that is where such a light could come on:
above a narrow bed where a girl and a boy
take themselves perhaps for the first time out of time.

The Apple Tree

I remember this tree,
its white flowers all unfallen.
It's the fall, the unfallen apples
hold their brightness
a little longer into the blue air, hold the idea
that they can be brighter.

We create without turning,
without looking back, without ever
really knowing we create.
Having tasted
the first flower of the first spring
we go on,
we don't turn again
until we touch the last flower of the last spring.

And that day, fondling
each grain one more time, like the neck of the hourglass,
we die
of the return-streaming of everything we have lived.

When the fallen apple rolls
into the grass, the apple worm
stops, then goes
all the way through and looks out
at the creation unopposed, the world
made entirely of lovers.

Or else there is no such thing as memory,
or else there are only the empty branches,
only the blossoms upon them,
only the apples,
that still grow full,
that still fail into brightness,
that still invent past their own decay the hope
they can be brighter,
that still
that still

The one who holds still and looks out,
alone
of all of us, may die mostly of happiness.

A Milk Bottle

A tiny creature slides
through the tide pool, holding up
its little fortress foretelling
our tragedies; another clamps
itself down to the stone. A sea anemone
sucks at my finger, mildly, I can just
feel it, though it may mean to kill—no,
it might say, to use me to receive
more life. All these creatures
even half made of stone thrill
to altered existences. As we do ourselves,
who advance so far, then stop, then creep
a little, stop, then gasp—breath
is the bright shell
of the life-wish encasing us—gasp
it all in again, on seeing that
any time would be OK
to disappear back into all things—as when
lovers wake up at night and see
the other is tearful and think, *Yes,*
but it doesn't matter, already
we will have lived forever. Yes,
if we could do that: separate
time from happiness, skim off
the molecules scattered
throughout our flesh that remember,
fling them at non-conscious things,

who may always have craved them ... It's funny,
I seem actually to remember a certain
quart of milk that has just finished
clinking against one of its brethren
in the milkman's great hand and stands
freeing itself from itself on the rotting
doorstep in Pawtucket in 1932; and is then
picked up and taken indoors
by one in whom time hasn't yet
woven its tangles. The bottle
will of course have shattered by now
in the decay of its music,
the sea eagle have rung
its glass voice back down into the sea
the sea's creatures transfigure over and over.
Look, around us the meantime has begun overflowing.
In every direction its own almost-invisibility
Streams and sparkles over everything.

Flying Home

1

Flying home, looking about
in this swollen airplane, every seat
of it squashed full with one of us,
it occurs to me I might be one of the lucky ones
in this planeload of the species;

for earlier,
in the airport men's room, seeing
the middleaged men my age,
as they washed their hands after touching
their penises—when it might have been more in accord
with the lost order to wash first, then touch—
peer into the mirror
and then stand back, as if asking, who is this?

Looking around, I could only think
that one looks relieved to be getting away,
that one dreads going where he goes.
As for me, at the very same moment
I feel regret at leaving
and happiness to be flying home.

2

Very likely she has always understood
what I have slowly learned

and which only now, after being about as far away
as one can get on this globe, almost
as far as thoughts can carry—yet still in her presence,
still surrounded not so much by reminders of her
as by things she had already reminded me of,
cast forward and waiting—can I try to express:

that while many good things are easy, love is hard,
because it is first of all a power,
its own power,
and must keep making its way forward, from night
into day, from transcending union forward into difficult day.

3

And as the plane starts its descent, it comes to me,
that once the lover
recognizes the other, knows for the first time
what is most to be valued in another,
from then on, love is very much like courage,
perhaps it *is* courage, and even
perhaps
only courage. Squashed
out of old selves, smearing the darkness
of expectation across experience, all of us little
thinkers it brings home having similar thoughts
of landing to the imponderable world,
the transcontinental airliner,

resisting its huge weight down, comes in almost lightly,
to where
with sudden, tiny, white puffs and long, black, rubberish smears
all its tires know the home ground.

The Past

for Inés

PART I

The Road Between Here and There

Here I heard the snorting of hogs trying to re-enter the underearth.

Here I came into the curve too fast, on ice, touched the brake
pedal and sailed into the pasture.

Here I stopped the car and snoozed while two small children
crawled all over me.

Here I reread *Moby Dick*, skipping big chunks, skimming others,
in a single day, while Maud and Fergus fished.

Here I abandoned the car because of a clonk in the motor and
hitchhiked (which in those days in Vermont meant walking
the whole way with a limp) all the way to a garage, where I
passed the afternoon with ex-loggers who had stopped by to
oil the joints of their artificial limbs and talk.

Here a barn burned down to the snow. "Friction," one of the ex-
loggers said. "Friction?" "Yup, the mortgage, rubbin' against
the insurance policy."

Here I went eighty but was in no danger of arrest, for I was blessed-
speeding, trying to get home to see my children before they
slept.

Here I bought speckled brown eggs with bits of straw shitted to
them.

Here I brought home in the back seat two piglets who rummaged
around inside the burlap sack like pregnancy itself.

Here I heard again on the car radio a Handel concerto transcribed
for harp and lute, which Inés played to me the first time,
making me want to drive after it and hear it forever.

Here I sat on a boulder by the winter-steaming river and put my
head in my hands and considered time—which is next to

nothing, merely what vanishes, and yet can make one's elbows nearly pierce one's thighs.

Here I forgot how to sing in the old way and listened to the frogs at dusk.

Here the local fortune teller took my hand and said, "What is still possible is inspired work, faithfulness to a few, and a last love, which, being last, will be like looking up and seeing the parachute turning into a shower of gold."

Here is the chimney standing up by itself and falling down, which tells you you approach the end of the road between here and there.

Here I arrive there.

Here I must turn around and go back and on the way back look carefully to left and to right.

For when the spaces along the road between here and there are all used up, that's it.

The Angel

This angel, who mediates between us
and the world underneath us, trots ahead
so cheerfully. Now and then she bends
her spine down hard, like a dowser's branch,
over some, to her, well-known splashing spot
of holy water, of which she herself in turn
carefully besoms out a thrifty sprinkle.
Trotting ahead again, she scribbles her spine's
continuation into immaterial et cetera,
thus signaling that it is safe for us now
to go vertically wagging our legs
across the ups and downs under which
lie ancestors dog-toothed millennia ago into oblivion.
Tonight she will crouch at the hearth,
where demons' breaths flutter up among the logs,
gnawing a freshly unearthed bone — of a dog,
it could be — making logs and bone
cry through the room, *crack splinter groan.*

Middle of the Night

A telephone rings through the wall.
Nobody answers. Exactly how
the mouth shapes itself inside
when saying the word "gold" is what sleep
would be like if one were happy.
So Kenny Hardman and George Sykes
called "Gaw-way-ay!" at the back
of the house. If I didn't come out
they would call until nightfall,
like summer insects. Or like
the pay phone at the abandoned
filling station, which sometimes
rang, off and on, an entire day.
The final yawn before one sleeps sounds
like the word "yes" said too many times,
too rapidly. On the landing
she turned and looked back. Something
in her of the sea turtle heavy with eggs,
looking back at the sea. The shocking dark
of her eyes awakened in me
an affirmative fire. It would have hurt
to walk away, just as it would bewilder
a mouth at certain moments in life to say "no."

Conception

Having crowed the seed
of the child of his heart
into the egg of the child
of her heart, in the dark
middle of the night, as cocks
sometimes cry out to a light
not yet visible to the rest,
and lying there with cock
shrugging its way out of her,
and rising back through phases
of identity, he hears her
say, "Yes, I am two now,
and with you, three."

The Sow Piglet's Escapes

When the little sow piglet squirmed free,
Gus and I ran her all the way down to the swamp
and lunged and floundered and fell full-length
on our bellies stretching for her, and got her,
and lay there, all three shining with swamp slime,
she yelping, I laughing, Gus gasping and gasping.
It was then I knew he would die soon.
She made her second escape on the one day
when she was big enough to dig an escape hole
and still small enough to squeeze through it.
Every day I took a bucket of meal up to her plot
of rooted-up ground in the woods, until
one day there she stood, waiting for me,
the wild beast evidently all mealed out of her.
She trotted over and let me stroke her back
and, dribbling corn down her chin, put up her little worried face
as if to remind me not to forget to recapture her,
though, really, a pig's special alertness to death
ought to have told her: in Sheffield the *dolce vita*
leads to the Lyndonville butcher. When I seized her
she wriggled hard and cried *oui oui oui* all the way home.

The Olive Wood Fire

When Fergus woke crying at night,
I would carry him from his crib
to the rocking chair and sit holding him
before the fire of thousand-year-old olive wood.
Sometimes, for reasons I never knew
and he has forgotten, even after his bottle the big tears
would keep on rolling down his big cheeks
—the left cheek always more brilliant than the right—
and we would sit, some nights for hours, rocking
in the light eking itself out of the ancient wood,
and hold each other against the darkness,
his close behind and far away in the future,
mine I imagined all around.
One such time, fallen half-asleep myself,
I thought I heard a scream
—a flier crying out in horror
as he dropped fire on he didn't know what or whom,
or else a child thus set aflame—
and sat up alert. The olive wood fire
had burned low. In my arms lay Fergus,
fast asleep, left cheek glowing, God.

Milk

When he pulls back on the oars
slightly too large for him, the boat
surges forward, toward the island
where he picks up the milk bottle
the old man he's never seen
puts out each morning at the end of the dock;
toward the shore by the highway
where he sets down four empty
milk bottles and picks up four full
left by the milkman he's never seen;
toward the dock where he leaves
a full bottle for the old man;
and then homeward across water
around which the trees stand
right side up in the world
and upside down in the world under it
into which utterly still moments
are the doors childhood almost opens.

Lake Memphremagog

We loaf in our gray boat in the sunshine.
The Canadian Pacific freight following the shoreline sends a
　　racket of iron over Lake Memphremagog.
The children cast, the fishes do not bite.
They leap into the water and splash, the Memphremagog monster
　　does not bite.
In the center of Newport, the train blows, one after one, all its five
　　horns.
I think I astonished my cheeks with the amount of tears one child
　　can cry.
Those nights now lie almost farther away than memory goes.
All the elsewheres, as the train's cries fade, fade.
Our boat lies very still in the Memphremagog water, and it's still.
Here everybody is OK.
I am fifty. The children are just little ones.

The Man Splitting Wood in the Daybreak

The man splitting wood in the daybreak
looks strong, as though, if one weakened,
one could turn to him and he would help.
Gus Newland was strong. When he split wood
he struck hard, flashing the bright steel
through the air so hard the hard maple
leapt apart, as it's feared marriages will do
in countries reluctant to permit divorce,
and even willow, which, though stacked
to dry a full year, on being split
actually weeps—totem wood, therefore,
to the married-until-death—sunders
with many little lip-wetting gasp-noises.
But Gus is dead. We could turn to our fathers,
but they help us only by the unperplexed
looking-back of the numerals cut into headstones.
Or to our mothers, whose love, so devastated,
can't, even in spring, break through the hard earth.
Our spouses weaken at the same rate we do.
We have to hold our children up to lean on them.
Everyone who could help goes or hasn't arrived.
What about the man splitting wood in the daybreak,
who looked strong? That was years ago. That was me.

The Frog Pond

In those first years I came down
often to the frog pond—once called,
before the earthen dam eroded,
the farm pond—to bathe, wading out
and standing on a rock up to my knees
in pond water, which I sauce-panned over me—
and doing it quickly because of the leeches,
who need but minutes to know you're there—
or to read the mail or to scribble
or to loaf and think, sometimes
of the future, while the one deerfly
that torments whoever walks out in Vermont
in July—smack it dead as often
as one will—orbited about my head.
Then the beavers arrived, the waters rose,
and the frog pond became the beaver pond.
A year later a sunken rowboat surfaced,
with sheet metal nailed all around it
to hold the hull boards in place
while they rotted. The four
of us would oar, pole, and bail
a few feet above the underwater green bank
where a man used to sit and think
and look up and seem to see four people
up here oaring and poling and bailing
above him: the man *seems* happy,
the two children laugh and splash,

a slight shadow crosses the woman's face.
Then one spring the beavers disappeared—
trapped off, or else because of gnawing down
all the edible trees—and soon this pond,
and the next, and the one after that,
will flow off, leaving behind its print
in the woods, a sudden green meadow
with gleams of sky meandering through it.
The man who lies propped up
on an elbow, scribbling, will be older
and will remember the pond as it was then,
writhing with leeches and overflown
by the straight blue bodies of dragonflies,
and will think of small children
grown up and of true love broken
and will sit up abruptly and swat
the hard-biting deerfly on his head,
crushing it into his hair, as he has done before.

The Old Life

The waves collapsed into themselves
with heavy rumbles in the darkness
and the soprano shingle whistled
gravely its way back into the sea.
When the moon came from behind clouds
its white full-moon's light
lightly oiled the little beach stones
back into silence. We stood
among shatterings, glitterings,
the brilliance. And now it happens
another lifetime is up for us,
another life is upon us.
What's left is what is left
of the whole absolutely love-time.

PART II

Prayer

Whatever happens. Whatever
what is is is what
I want. Only that. But that.

The Ferry Stopping at MacMahon's Point

It comes vigorously in,
nudges the jetty and ties up,
the usually ill-tossed line tossed twice,
presses by engine pressure against
the pilings for a half-minute,
backs out, turns, and prow lifted
like the head of a swimming dog,
makes for the Lavender Bay jetty.

Mount Fuji at Daybreak

From the Fuji-view stand made of cinder block
a crow watches Fuji rise into daybreak.
Trash smoke light-blues the exhausted valley.
Hot-spring steam blows up out of steam holes.
Up the road leaving town a tanker truck groans.
An electric bullhorn starts crackling messages
to workers coming early out of their doors.
From the cinder block Fuji-view stand the crow
flies off repeating the round vowel "ah!"
to the mountain now risen bright into daybreak,
or else, in another mood, "ha! ha! ha!"

Break of Day

He turns the light on, lights
the cigarette, goes out on the porch,
chainsaws a block of green wood down the grain,
chucks the pieces into the box stove,
pours in kerosene, tosses in the match
he has set fire to the next cigarette with,
stands back while the creosote-lined, sheet-
metal rust-lengths shudder but just barely
manage to direct the *cawhoosh* in the stove —
which sucks in ash motes through gaps
at the bottom and glares out fire blaze
through overburn-cracks at the top —
all the way to the roof and up out through into
the still starry sky starting to lighten,
sits down to a bowl of crackers and bluish milk
in which reflections of a 40-watt ceiling bulb
appear and disappear, eats, contemplates
an atmosphere containing kerosene stink,
chainsaw smoke, chainsmoke, wood smoke, wood heat,
gleams of the 40-watt ceiling bulb bobbing in blue milk.

Farm Picture

Black earth
turned up, clods
shining on their
western sides, grass
sprouting on top
of bales of spoiled
hay, an old
farmer bent far
over, like *Australopithecus
robustus*, carrying two dented
pails of water out
to the hen yard.

Some Song

On a stoop
the old man
is drinking him
some beer,
the boy in
his yellow shirt
is playing
him some banjo tune,
the old fellow
hasn't any
teeth, the boy
sings him then
some song.

Coinaliste

She can drink from a beer bottle.
She can light a cigar and sneeze out the match.
She can drag on it so hard the end blazes.
She can inhale without coughing.
She can blow a smoke ring or two.
She can withdraw and introspect.

She can play the nose flute: f# with lower hole unstopped; a with
    both holes unstopped; c# with both stopped: the tonic, the
    mediant, the dominant of the chord of F# major.
She can suck the whole instrument inside, where it continues to
    sing and cry.
She can speak a pouting, pidgin blabber.

She can clench on the ictus and moan on the arsis but cannot
    come on the thesis.
She can wink and throw French kisses.
She can motherly-kiss the fuzzy cheeks of young sailors.
She can pick up the money they toss, including the dollar bills.
She can count but not give change.
She can smile.

Driftwood from a Ship

It is the white of faces from which the sunburn has been scared
away.
It has the rounded shoulders of one who fears he will pass the rest
of his days alone.
The black residue inside the line of nine nail holes—three close
together, three far apart, three close together—is the memory
hammered just in case of shipwreck into those vanishing
places.
A carpenter's plane's long, misericording *shhhhhhhhh*'s long ago
soothed away the halo-segments that a circular saw longer ago
tormented across it.
The pebbles it rubs itself across fuzz up all over it a first beard,
white from the start.
The grain cherishes the predicament of the Norway spruce, which
has a trunk that rises and boughs that droop.
Its destiny, which is to disappear, could be accomplished when a
beachcomber extracts its heat, leaving the smoke and ashes;
or in the normal way, through a combination of irritation and
evanescence.

Fire in Luna Park

The screaming produced by the great fright machines—
one like a dough beater that lifts, whirls, plunges the victims
        strapped in its arms,
one a huge fluted pan that tries to fling its passengers off the earth,
one that holds its riders upside down and pummels them until
        they pour out their screams freely,
and above them the roller coaster, creeping seemingly lost among
        its struts and braces,
and under them the Ghost Train that jerks through dark tunnels
        here and there suddenly lighted by fluorescent bones—
has fallen still today.

To us who live on Lavender Bay,
once Hulk Bay, before that probably few if any now know what,
it seemed the same easily frightened, big-lunged screamer cried
        out in mock terror each night across the water, and we hardly
        heard or took notice.
But last night shrieks of true terror pierced through our laughter,
        and kept at it, until we sat up startled.

The Ghost Train, now carrying seven souls and the baffled grief of
        families,
has no special destination,
but, looking for forgetfulness, must thrust forward, twist, backtrack
        through the natural world,
where all are born, all suffer, and many scream,
and no one is healed but gathered and used again.

The Geese

As soon as they come over the peak
into the Connecticut Valley and espy the river
that they will follow until nightfall,
bodies, or cells, begin to tumble
between the streamers of their formation,
thinning the left, thickening the right,
until like a snowplowing skier the flock shifts weight
and shaking up its inner equipoise
turns, and yahonks and spirit-cries
toward the flow of light spelled
into the river's windings eons ago,
each body flashing white against
the white sky when the wings lift,
and black when they fall, the invisible
continuously perforating the visible—
and trembles away, to vanish, but before that
to semi-vanish, as a mirage or deepest
desire does when it gets the right
distance from us and becomes rhythmic.

The Shroud

Lifted by its tuft
of angel hairs, a milkweed
seed rises and dips
across a meadow, chalking
in outline the rhythms
wavering through air all along.
Spinus tristis, who expends
his days transfiguring gold
back into sod, sinks and soars,
following the same undulations.
What immense coat or shroud
that can wrap the whole earth
are these golden needles
stitching at so restlessly?
When will it ever be finished?

PART III

Chamberlain's Porch

On three sides of the stretcher bed
where I half sleep, rainwater runs down
boughs all broken out in buds out there
in the world that the porch screen crisscrosses
into tiny, very perishable rectangles.
Rain putters down on wood shingles,
now smattering, becoming a language,
now slackening, making kissing sounds
which some would memorize into the grave.
It seems the mechanism driving the inner
pluckings of things, which lives by crescendo,
here stops and tries out low-key backward variations
on a cedar-shingled porch roof in Connecticut.

Cemetery Angels

On these cold days
they stand over
our dead, who will
erupt into flower as soon
as memory and human shape
rot out of them, each bent
forward and with wings
partly opened as though
warming itself at a fire.

December Day in Honolulu

This day, twice as long as the same day in Sheffield, Vermont,
    where by five the stars come out,
gives the postman opportunity to boggle the bell thrice.
First, a letter from Providence lamenting the "siege against
    poets"—Wright, Rukeyser, Hayden.
Next, Richard Hugo's memoir of James Wright.
Last, around the time of stars in Sheffield, a package holding four
    glass doorknobs packed in a *New York Times* of a year ago,
    which Muriel Rukeyser had sea-mailed to me, in explanation
    of those somewhat alarming words she would whisper
    whenever we met: "Galway, I have your doorknobs."
The wail of a cat in heat breaks in, the voice of propagation itself:
This one or that one dies but never the singer: whether in Honolulu
    in its humid mornings or New York in its unbreathable dusk or
    Sheffield now dark but for chimney sparks dying into the
    crowded heaven, one singer falls and the next steps into the
    empty place and sings...
The cat's next wail comes more heavily, as if from a longer inner
    distance.
It could be it's just a very old cat, singing its last appearance in the
    magic circle of a trash can lid, perhaps from its final life
    trying to cry back the first life's first, irreplaceable lover,
    before turning totally faithful forever.

On the Oregon Coast

In memoriam Richard Hugo

Six or seven rows of waves struggle landward.
The wind batters a pewtery sheen on the valleys between them.
Much of each wave making its way in gets blown back out to sea.
The bass rumble of sea stones audible under their outrush itself
      blows out to sea.
A log maybe thirty feet long and six across at the fat end gets up
      and trundles down the beach, using its two ends like feet.
Like a dog fetching a stick, it flops unhesitatingly into the water.
An enormous wave at once sends it wallowing back up the beach.
It comes to rest among other lost logs, almost panting.
Sure enough, in a few minutes it trundles down the beach again.
The last time I was on this coast I had dinner with Richard Hugo
      north of here, in a restaurant over the sea.
The conversation came around to personification.
We agreed that eighteenth- and nineteenth-century poets almost
      had to personify, it was like mouth-to-mouth resuscitation, the
      only way they could think up to keep the world from
      becoming dead matter.
And that as post-Darwinians it was up to us to anthropomorphize
      the world less and animalize, vegetablize, and mineralize
      ourselves more.
We didn't know if pre-Darwinian language would let us.
Our talk turned to James Wright, how his confabulations with
      reptiles, spiders, and insects drifted him back through the
      evolutionary stages.
When a group of people get up from a table, the table doesn't
      know which way any of them will go.

James Wright went back to the end. So did Richard Hugo.
The waves swaffing in burst up through their crests and fly very
    brilliant back out to sea.
The log gets up once again, rolls and bounces down the beach,
    plunges as though for good into the water.

Last Holy Fragrance

In memoriam James Wright

When by first light I went out
from the last house on the chemin de Riou
to start up the cistern pump, I saw him,
mumbling into his notebook
while the valley awakened: a cock
called full force, a car's gears
mis-shifted, a dog made feeble yaps.
The next winter in Mt. Sinai,
tufted with the stubble that sticks out
of chins on skid row in St. Paul,
Minnesota, he handed me the poem
of that Vence morning. Many times since,
I have said it and each time I have heard
his voice saying it under mine,
and in fact in those auditoriums
that don't let you hear yourself, sometimes
I have heard *only* his voice, surprising language
a little with the mourning
that goes on inside it, for what it names.
And in the droning mutter I remember
sometimes his eyes would pop,
as he read, showing the whites
when his own poems startled him.
.
"How am I ever going to be able to say this?
The truth is there is something terrible,
almost unspeakably terrible in our lives,

and it demands respect, and, for some reason
that seems to me quite insane, it doesn't hate us.
There, you see? Every time I try
to write it down it comes out gibberish."

He lies back fast asleep in the airplane seat.
Under his eyelids consciousness flickers.
A computation: the difference, figured
in a flash, between what has been lived
and what remains to be. He dreams perhaps
of whittling a root, transfiguring it
by subtraction—of whatever it is in roots
that makes them cling—perhaps into
a curled up, oriental death's body
mummified into the memories of last visitors.
Even asleep his face sweats. SS
torturers start working Cagney over.
He knows he will crack and spill
the invasion plans. When he hears
the rumbling of B-29s
come to shut his mouth, he cracks
 a grin. When the bombs explode
he madly laughs. Sitting up,
he peers out the small, round window
to see if we might be coming in too low,
ready himself to laugh among the screams.

For this poet, the blessed moment
was not only at the end, in Fano, in spring,
where, with his beloved Annie,

just before returning home to die,
he got well, but also at first,
forty years earlier, by the Ohio,
where he sat and watched it
flow, and flowed himself inside it,
humming and lulling first beginnings
of poems that would heal himself
but also everybody, including those
who lie on sidewalks, like dropped
flowers waiting to be lady slippered
into first perfume or last stink.

The computation darkens.
Again and again it used to show
plenty of time. Now, even on
the abacus of the rosary, or the petals,
hushed to the tabletop, of roses,
which we mortal augurers figure
and refigure things out on our
incredulous infinity of times,
it comes out: a negative number.
Fear, the potion of death, is yet
a love derivative, and some terrible
pinch of it must be added one
way or another to bring back
our will to cling.

Near where it first forms,
the Ohio stops in its bed
and baptizes under ice

its creatures, as well as the boy sitting soon
in nobody's memory some days downriver.
He went away, three-quarters
whittled root of silenus wood, taking
a path that, had it vanished,
we could imagine keeps going, toward a place
where he waits to rise again
into the religion of the idolatry
of the things of earth graven
their moment into being-born-and-dying.

The path ends where a white rose
lies on top of its shadow in Martin's Ferry,
Ohio, let drop by a child too stunned
by dead bells pounding through sunlight
to hold it, or anything, or anyone, tight
that day, giving up its last holy fragrance
into this ending-time, when the earth
lets itself be shoveled open to take in a body.
It will be a long time before anyone comes
who can lull the words he will now not again use
—words which, now he has gone, turn this way and that—
hum and inveigle them to press up against, shape
themselves by, know, true-love, and idolize.

The Past

A chair under one arm,
a desktop under the other,
the same Smith-Corona
on my back I even now batter
words into visibility with,
I would walk miles,
assemble my writing stall,
type all day, many sheets
of prose and verse later
to blow away, while gulls,
sometimes a sightseeing plane,
turned overhead. The lean-
to of driftwood that thirty-
three-and-a-third years back
I put up on this spot
leans down all the way.
Its driftwood re-drifts.
Spray jumps and blows.
A few gulls fly that way,
a few this. One duck
whettles out to sea
in straight flight.
As for the Quonset hut
I broke into without breaking it
when the storms came, it too
has gone, swept out to sea, burned up,
buried under, torn down.

Too bad. But for me not all
that bad. For of the four
possibilities—from *me-and-it-*
still-here to *it-and-me-*
both-gone—this one, *me-here-*
it-gone, is second best,
and will do, for me, for now.
But I wanted to sit at the table again
and look up and see the sea spray
and beach grass happy together.
I wanted to remember
the dingy, sprouted potatoes,
the Portuguese bread, the Bokar coffee,
the dyed oranges far from home,
the water tasting of eroded aluminum,
the kerosene stench. The front
steps where I watched
the elation in the poverty grass,
when the wind blew. In a letter
that cast itself down in General
Delivery, Provincetown, my friend
and mentor warned, "Don't lose
all touch with humankind." One day
while all around gulls gave
exhausted screams, the wind
put a sudden sheen or flatness
like spiritual quietness across the water.
Now two waves of the North Atlantic
roll landward side by side,
converge, ripple into one,

rush up the beach, making me
jump back, and sink away under
white bubbles all suddenly
popping away at once. Here
waves slap not in time but in
evanescence, a rhythmless medium.
Mere comings, mere goings. Though now
there's somewhat less coming
in the comings and more
going in the goings. Between
the two straggles a wandering
thread of sea litter
along the beach. So you see,
to reach the past is a snap. A snap
of the sea and a third of a century's
gone. All nothing. Or all all,
if that sounds more faithful. But anyway
vanished. The work of
whoziwhatzit—Zeit ... Zman ... Chas ...
whatever ... Whichever
you strike with the desperate tongue coughs up
a deadened sound, as though
the thing itself were fake; or unutterable.

First Day of the Future

They always seem to come up
on the future, these cold, earthly dawns;
the whiteness and the blackness
make the flesh shiver as though starting to break.
But so far it's just another day they illuminate
of the permanent present. Except for today.
A motorboat sets out across the bay,
a transfiguring spirit, its little puffy gasps
of disintegration collected
and hymned out in a pure purr of dominion.
In the stillness again the shore lights remember
the dimensions of the black water.
I don't know about this new life.
Even though I burned the ashes of its flag
and ate the ticket that would have conscripted me into its ranks
    forever
and squandered my talents composing my emigration papers,
I think I want to go back now and live again in the present time,
    back there
where someone milks a cow and jets of intensest nourishment go
    squawking into a pail,
where someone is hammering, a bit of steel at the end of a stick
    hitting a bit of steel, in the archaic stillness of an afternoon,
or somebody else saws a board, back and forth, like hard labor
in the lungs of one who refuses to come to the very end.
But I guess I'm here. So I must take care. For here
one has to keep facing the right way, or one sees one dies, and one
    dies.

The Fundamental Project of Technology

"A flash! A white flash sparkled!"
    —Tatsuichiro Akizuki, *Concentric Circles of Death*

Under glass: glass dishes that changed
in color; pieces of transformed beer bottles;
a household iron; bundles of wire become solid
lumps of iron; a pair of pliers; a ring of skull-
bone fused to the inside of a helmet; eyeglasses
taken off the eyes of an eyewitness, without glass,
which vanished, when a white flash sparkled.

An old man, possibly a soldier back then,
now simply somebody who will die soon,
sucks at the cigarette dangling from his lip, peers
at the uniform, scorched, of some tiniest schoolboy,
sighs out bluish mists of his own ashes over
a pressed tin lunch box well crushed back then when
the word future first learned, in a white flash, to jerk tears.

On the bridge outside, in navy black, a group
of schoolchildren line up, hold it, grin at a flash-pop,
scatter like pigeons across grass, see a stranger, cry
hello! hello! hello! and soon *bye-bye! bye-bye! bye-bye!*
having pecked up the greetings that fell half unspoken
and the going-sayings that those who went the day
it happened a white flash sparkled did not get to say.

If all a city's faces were to shrink back all at once
from their skulls, would a new sound come into existence,
audible above moans eaves extract from wind that smooths

the grass on graves, or raspings heart's-blood greases still,
or wails infants trill born already skillful at the grandpa's rattle,
or infra-screams bitter-knowledge's speechlessness
memorized, at that white flash, inside closed-forever mouths?

To de-animalize human mentality, and at the same time to
     purge it
of unfavorable evolutionary characteristics, in particular
the foreknowledge of death, which terrorizes the contents
of skulls, is the fundamental project of technology;
however, *pseudologica fantastica*'s mechanisms require
to establish deathlessness it is necessary to eliminate
those who die; a task become conceivable, when a white flash
     sparkled.

Unlike the trees of home, which continuously evaporate
along the skyline, these trees have been enticed down
into eternity here. No one can say which gods they enshrine.
Does it matter? Awareness of ignorance is as devout
as knowledge of knowledge. Or more so. Even though not
     knowing,
sometimes we weep, from surplus of gratitude, even though
     knowing,
twice already on earth sparkled a flash, a white flash.

The children go away. By nature they do. And by memory,
in scorched uniforms, holding tiny crushed lunch tins.
All the ecstasy-groans of each night call them back, satori
their ghostliness back into the ashes, in the momentary shrines,
the thankfulness of arms, from which they will go
again and again, until the day flashes and no one lives
to look back and say, a flash, a white flash sparkled.

The Waking

What has just happened between the lovers,
who lie now in love-sleep under the owls' calls,
call, answer, back and forth, and so on,
until one, calling faster, overtakes the other
and the two whoo together in a single
shimmering harmonic, is called "lovemaking."
Lovers who come exalted to their trysts,
who approach from opposite directions
through the pines, along a path by the sea,
meet, embrace, go up from the sea,
lie crushed into each other under
the sky half-golden, half deep-blueing
its moon and stars into shining, know
they don't "make" love, but are earth-creatures
who live and—here maybe no other word will do—
fuck one another forever if possible across the stars.
An ancient word, formed perhaps before
sacred and profane had split apart
when the tongue, like a flame
in the mouth, lighted each word
as it was spoken, to remind it
to remember; as when flamingos
change feeding places on a marsh,
and there is a moment, after the first to fly
puts its head into the water in the new place
and before in the old place the last
lifts up its head to see the rest have flown,

when, scattered with pink bodies, the sky
is one vast remembering. They still hear,
in sleep, the steady crushing and uncrushing
of bedsprings; they imagine a sonata in which
violins' lines draw the writhings and shiftings.
They lie with heads touching, thinking
themselves back across the blackness.
When dawn comes their bodies re-form
into two heaps of golden matter sieved
out of the night. The bed, caressed threadbare,
worn almost away, is now more than ever
the place where such light as humans
shine with seeps up into us. The eyelids,
which love the eyes and lie on them to sleep,
open. *This is a bed. That is a fireplace.*
That is last morning's breakfast tray
which nobody has yet bothered to take away.
This face, too alive with feeling to survive past
the world in which it is said, "Ni vous
sans moi, ni moi sans vous," so unguarded
that this day might be breaking in the Middle Ages,
is the illusion fate's randomness chooses
to beam into existence, now, on this pillow.
In a ray of sun the lovers see motes cross,
mingle, collide, lose their way, in this puff
of ecstatic dust. Tears overfill their eyes,
wet their faces, then drain quickly away
into their smiles. One leg hangs off the bed.
He is still inside her. His big toe
sticks into the pot of strawberry jam. "Oh migod!"

They kiss while laughing and hit teeth
and remember they are bones and laugh
naturally again. The feeling, perhaps
it is only a feeling, perhaps mostly due
to living only in the overlapping lifetimes
of dying things, that time starts up again,
comes over them. They put on clothes,
go out. For a few moments longer
are still in their elsewhere, beside a river,
their arms around each other, in the aura
earth has when it remembers its former beauty.
An ambulance sirens a bandage-stiffened
body toward St. Vincent's; a police car
running the red lights parodies
in high pitch the owls of paradise. So the lovers
enter the ordinary day the ordinary world
providentially provides. Their pockets ring.
Good. For now askers and beggarmen
come up to them needing change for breakfast.

That Silent Evening

I will go back to that silent evening
when we lay together and talked in low, silent voices,
while outside slow lumps of soft snow
fell, hushing as they got near the ground,
with a fire in the room, in which centuries
of tree went up in continuous ghost-giving-up,
without a crackle, into morning light.
When we got home we turned and looked back
at our tracks twining out of the woods,
where the branches we brushed against let fall
puffs of sparkling snow, quickly, in silence,
like stolen kisses, and where the *scritch scritch scritch*
among the trees, which is the sound that dies
inside the sparks from the wedge when a sledge
hits it off center telling everything inside
it is fire, jumped to a black branch, puffed up
but without arms and so to our eyes lonesome,
and yet also—how can we know this?—*happy!*
in shape of chickadee. Lying still in snow,
not iron-willed, like railroad tracks, willing
not to meet until heaven, but here and there
treading slubby kissing stops, our tracks wobble
across the snow their long, interrupted scratch.
So many things that happen here are little more,
if even that, than a scratch. Words in our mouths
are almost ready, already, to bandage the one
whom the *scritch scritch scritch*, meaning *if how when*

we might lose each other, scratches scratches scratches
from this moment to that. Then I will go back
to that silent evening, when the past just managed
to overlap the future, if only by a trace,
and the light doubled and cast
through the dark the sparkling that heavened the earth.

The Seekonk Woods

When first I walked here I hobbled
along ties set too close together
for a boy to step easily on each.
I thought my stride one day
would reach every other and from then on
I would walk in time with the way
toward that Lobachevskian haze
up ahead where the two rails meet.
Here we put down our pennies, dark,
on shined steel; they trembled, fell still;
then the locomotive out of Attleboro
rattling its berserk wheel-rods into perfect circles,
brightened them into wafers, the way a fork
mashes into view the inner light of a carrot
in a stew. In this late March sunshine,
crossing the trees at the angle of a bow
when it effleurages out of the chanterelle
the C three octaves above middle C,
the vertical birthwood remembers
its ascent lines, shrunken by half, exactly
back down, each tree on its fallen summer.
Back then, these rocks often asked
blood offerings—but this one, once, asked bone,
the time Billy Wallace tripped and broke out
his front teeth. Fitted with gold replicas,
he asked, speaking more brightly, "What good
are golden teeth, given what we've got

to eat?" Nebuchadnezzar
spent seven years down on all fours
eating vetch and alfalfa, ruminating
the mouth-feel of "bloom" and "wither,"
until he was whole. If you
held a grass blade between both thumbs
and blew hard you could blurt a shriek
out of it—like that beseeching leaves oaks
didn't drop last winter just now scratch
on a breeze. Maybe Billy, lured
by bones' memory, comes back
sometimes, too, to the Seekonk Woods,
to stand in the past and just look at it.
Here he might kneel, studying this clump of grass,
as a god might inspect the strands of a human sneeze
that percusses through. Or he might stray
into the now untrafficked whistling-lanes
of the mourning doves, who used to call and call
into the future, and give a start, as though,
this very minute, by awful coincidence,
they reach it. And at last traipse off
down the tracks, with arrhythmic gait,
as wanderers must do once they realize:
the over-the-unknown route, too, ends up
where time wants. On this spot
I skinned the muskrat. The musk breezed away.
I buried the rat. Of the fur
I made a hat, which as soon as put on
began to rot off, causing my scalp to crawl.
In circles, of course, keeping to the skull.

One day could this scrap of damp skin
crawl all the way off, and the whole organism
follow? To do what? Effuse with musk,
or rot with rat? When, a quarter-
turn after the sun, the half-moon,
too, goes down and we find ourselves
in the night's night, then somewhere
hereabouts in the dark must be death.
Knowledge of it beforehand is surely among
existence's most spectacular feats—and yet right here,
on this ordinary afternoon, in these woods,
with a name meaning "black goose" in Wampanoag,
or in modern Seekonkese, "slob blowing fat nose,"
this unlikely event happens—a creature
walking the tracks knows it will come.
Then too long to touch every tie, his stride
is now just too short to reach every other,
and so he is to be still the wanderer, the hirtle
of too much replaced by the common limp
of too little. But he almost got there.
Almost stepped in consonance with the liturgical,
sleeping gods' snores you can hear humming up
from former times inside the ties. He almost
set foot in that border zone where what follows
blows back, shimmering everything, making
walking like sleepwalking, railroad tracks
a country lane on a spring morning,
on which a man, limping but blissful,
makes his way homeward, his lips, suppled
by kissing to bunch up like that, blowing

these short strands of hollowed-out air,
haunted by future, into a tune on the tracks.
I think I'm about to be shocked awake.
As I was in childhood, when I battered myself
back to my senses against a closed door,
or woke up hanging out of an upstairs window.
Somnambulism was my attempt to slip
under cover of nightmare across no father's land
and embrace a phantasm. If only
I had found a way to enter his hard time
served at labor by day, by night in solitary,
and put my arms around him in reality,
I might not now be remaking him
in memory still; anti-alchemizing bass kettle's
golden reverberations back down
to hair, flesh, blood, bone, the base metals.
I want to crawl face down in the fields
and graze on the wild strawberries, my clothes
stained pink, even for seven years
if I must, if they exist. I want to lie out
on my back under the thousand stars and think
my way up among them, through them,
and a little distance past them, and attain
a moment of absolute ignorance,
if I can, if human mentality lets us.
I have always intended to live forever;
but not until now, to live now. The moment
I have done one or the other, I here swear,
no one will have to drag me , I'll come
but never will I agree to burn my words.

The poplar logs creosoted asleep under the tracks
have stopped snoring. Maybe they've
already waked up. The bow saws at G.
An oak leaf rattles on its tree. The rails
may never meet, O fellow Euclideans,
for you, for me. So what if we groan.
That's our noise. Laughter is our stuttering
in a language we can't speak yet. Behind,
the world made of wishes goes dark. Ahead,
if not now then never, shines what is.

ACKNOWLEDGMENTS

Many of the poems in this volume were originally published in the following magazines, journals, and books:

Body Rags

Choice: "Mango" and "Testament of the Thief"; *Colorado State Review:* "Getting the Mail"; *The Hudson Review:* "The Porcupine"; *The Minor Bird:* "The Falls"; *The Nation:* "Last Songs" and "Night in the Forest"; *The New Yorker:* "The Fossils" and "La Bagarède"; *The Paris Review:* "Another Night in the Ruins"; *Poetry:* "The Last River" (under the title "The Mystic River"), "The Correspondence School Instructor Says Goodbye to His Poetry Students," "The Poem," "In the Anse Galet Valley," "How Many Nights," and "In the Farmhouse"; *A Poetry Reading Against the Vietnam War:* "Vapor Trail Reflected in the Frog Pond"; *The Sixties:* "Going Home by Last Light" and "The Bear."

Mortal Acts, Mortal Words

The American Poetry Review: "Angling, a Day," "On the Tennis Court at Night," "The Last Hiding Places of Snow," and "The Sadness of Brothers"; *Chicago Review:* "The Still Time"; *Choice:* "After Making Love We Hear Footsteps"; *Country Journal:* "Kissing the Toad"; *Field:* "Looking at Your Face"; *Harper's Magazine:* "There Are Things I Tell to No One"; *Harvard Magazine:* "Blackberry Eating"; *Iowa Review:* "Fisherman"; *Kenyon Review:* "Goodbye" and "Lava"; *Mississippi Review:* "52 Oswald Street"; *Missouri Review:* "The

Apple"; *New England Review:* "In the Bamboo Hut"; *New Letters:* "Brother of My Heart"; *The New Republic:* "Les Invalides"; *The New Yorker:* "Daybreak," "Fergus Falling," "The Apple Tree," "The Choir," "The Gray Heron," "Saint Francis and the Sow," and "Wait"; *The New York Review of Books:* "Flying Home"; *The Paris Review:* "The Milk Bottle"; *The Three Rivers Poetry Journal:* "Memory of Wilmington."

The Past

The American Poetry Review: "The Fundamental Project of Technology," "On the Oregon Coast," and "The Waking"; *Antaeus:* "Conception," "December Day in Honolulu," "Driftwood from a Ship," and "The Man Splitting Wood in the Daybreak"; *Apparitions:* "Cemetery Angels" and "Farm Picture"; *The Atlantic:* "The Past"; *Kenyon Review:* "Fire in Luna Park" and "Last Holy Fragrance"; *Mother Jones:* "The Road Between Here and There"; *The Nation:* "Break of Day" and "Prayer"; *New Letters:* "The Olive Wood Fire"; *The New Yorker:* "First Day of the Future," "Middle of the Night," "The Seekonk Woods," and "The Shroud"; *The Paris Review:* "Chamberlain's Porch," "The Frog Pond," "The Geese," and "The Old Life"; *Scripsi:* "The Ferry Stopping at MacMahon's Point"; *Southwest Review:* "Milk"; *Verse:* "The Angel" and "The Sow Piglet's Escapes."

INDEX

GALWAY KINNELL is a former MacArthur fellow and has been the state poet of Vermont. In 1982 his *Selected Poems* won the Pulitzer Prize and the National Book Award. He has translated works of Bonnefoy, Lorca, Rilke, and Villon. Kinnell is Erich Maria Remarque Professor of Creative Writing at New York University. He lives in New York City and Vermont.